MW01173237

MEDICINAL MUSHROOMS

A Practical Guide to Healing Mushrooms

RICHARD BRAY

Published by *Monkey Publishing*
Edited by *Lili Marlene Booth*
Cover Design by *Diogo Lando*[1]
Graphic on Title Page:
Mis-Tery/Shutterstock.com

Printed by *Amazon*

1st Edition, published in 2020
© 2020 by Monkey Publishing
Lerchenstrasse 111
22767 Hamburg
Germany

ISBN: 9798670261661

All rights reserved, including the right to reproduce this book or portions thereof in any form whatsoever except for brief quotations in critical reviews or articles, without the prior written permission of the publisher.

---

[1] *Images: Moolkum, PattyPhoto, Tarapong Srichaiyos, Akepong Srichaichana, Jiang Zhongyan, mis-Tery/Shutterstock.com*

MONKEY PUBLISHING

OUR HAND-PICKED
BOOK SELECTION FOR YOU.

LEARN
SOMETHING NEW
EVERYDAY.

YOUR FREE BONUS

As a small token of thanks for buying this book, I am offering a free bonus gift exclusive to my readers. In this guide you`ll learn everything about herbs that can boost your immune system.

The guide is an excerpt from one of my bestselling books, *Natural Herbal Remedies: Herbal Medicine for Everyday Ailments,* which teaches you about healing herbs to improve your well-being.

If you want to learn more about herbal remedies, you can download the free bonus **www.herbalremedies.gr8.com**

DISCLAIMER

The information presented in this book is meant for educational purposes and does not replace professional medical advice from a health care practitioner. This text is not meant to diagnose or treat diseases. Mushrooms may cause adverse reactions; being included in this text does not mean they are safe for all to consume. The author and publisher of this book do not accept liability or responsibility for the use of mushrooms in treating health or medical issues. A person should always consult a health care practitioner before taking supplements and should disclose any currently being taken.

This is by no means a comprehensive guide to all potential medicinal mushrooms. It is a compilation of current research and recommended usages and does not cover all possibilities or concerns. There is a lot more research to be done, specifically around the best ways to ingest mushrooms and appropriate amounts. If the specific information you are looking for is not contained in this book, it likely means that there is not enough research yet or not enough evidence to support use. For example, many studies show that a specific mushroom has potential for treating cancer. Yet there are no resources available as to how much of that mushroom is needed to fight cancer effectively in humans.

This is still an area of immense study, and all the answers are not available as of yet.

reishi

Lion's Mane mushroom

Cordyceps

Chaga mushroom

Sophie_Rose/Shutterstock.com

TABLE OF CONTENT

CHAPTER 1

THE POWER OF MUSHROOMS

Melesandre/Shutterstock.com

For thousands of years, mushrooms have been used as food and medicine. There are over 14,000 species of mushrooms, and approximately 270 of them are identified as having potential medicinal benefits. These benefits include anti-cancer, anti-inflammatory, immune-system, depression relief, cholesterol inhibiting, and neurodegenerative disease treatment.

Because of the large number of mushroom types and the biological intricacies of each, there is no overarching statement that can be applied to them all. Each mushroom stands on its own with its specific medicinal properties. Some mushrooms are disease-specific, while others have more broad applications.

Our knowledge of these mushrooms mostly comes from the East Asian traditional medicinal practices that have been using them for centuries to assist in all manner of ailments, to prevent sickness, and even to cure diseases. Indigenous cultures across the world have long known the healing powers of mushrooms. Western medicine has only recently begun expressing interest, and there are still a lot of clinical studies that need to be done to prove scientifically that which ancient peoples have known for a long time.

The first major western discovery of powerful fungi was when Alexander Fleming accidentally found penicillin in 1928. Several current pharmaceutical medicines use mushroom or fungi sources in their compounds. Research is ongoing and increasingly prolific around mushrooms and their potential in treating serious diseases, like cancer, diabetes, and heart disease.

The interest in mushrooms as medicinal vehicles has reached such epic proportions because our current (western-style) medical system is struggling to provide safe and effective care. So many medications have undesirable and often serious side-effects. All too often, the drug a person takes for one disease causes another one. Mushrooms, over millennia, have been used to treat symptoms, cure diseases, and improve overall quality of life. Current research is finally beginning to catch up and demonstrate the true value of these natural commodities.

CHAPTER 2

EARLY USE OF MEDICINAL MUSHROOMS

For thousands of years, people across the globe have been using mushrooms for their medicinal properties. The uses range widely and are as varied as the types of mushrooms themselves. Hippocrates advocated the use of the amadou mushroom (*Fomes fomentarius*) as an anti-inflammatory. Reishi (*Ganoderma lucidum*) was used as far back as the 5th century by the alchemist Tao Hongjing. Even Otzi, the Ice Man, who lived around 3300 BCE, carried mushrooms in his pouch as he attempted to cross the Alps. Remnants of amadou and birch polypore, which is used to plaster wounds and fight infection, were discovered with his frozen body. Chaga has been used in Siberia and parts of North America for hundreds of years. Maitake is referenced as a treatment for stomach issues and to calm nerves in a Chinese text by Nong Ben Cao Jing, which was written between 200 BC and 200 AD.

In ancient Egypt, mushrooms were thought to be the "son of gods". The belief was that mushrooms arrived on lightning bolts and were only for the nobles and leaders to eat. Aztec culture ascribed sacred value to mushrooms. There, similar to Egyptian culture, the mushrooms were referred to as "the flesh of gods". They were eaten during holy rituals. Cultivation of mushrooms for culinary and medicinal purposes started thousands of years ago, primarily in Asia. Flammulina velutipes was cultivated as early as 800AD and Lentinula edodes (Shiitake) around 1000AD.

CHAPTER 3

BENEFITS OF MEDICINAL MUSHROOMS

The main benefit of medicinal mushrooms is their natural ability and the overall safety in using them. The side-effects with some are few and often very specific. Compared to the common medications that are prescribed by western doctors, the side-effects are negligible. The main issue with current medical drugs is not that they don't work; it is that they cause a myriad of other issues with long-term use. A person may start with one health issue, take prescribed medication for it, and end up with 2-3 other health problems due to the medication. This is not always a good strategy for treatment.

The mushrooms being studied for medicinal uses are generally safe to eat with minimal side-effects if any. Not all mushrooms are safe, and not all are medicinal, so it is important to follow the research and only ingest those known to be beneficial.

A second huge benefit to mushroom medicinals is that they cost less than other comparable medicines. If a person is educated in foraging, the mushrooms are free. Some mushrooms, like Pleurotus ostreatus (Oyster mushrooms) and Agaricus bisporus (Button mushrooms), are available for a minimal cost at the grocery store. There are types of mushrooms, some in this list, which are more expensive due to their rarity or the inability to commercially cultivate them. A lot depends on location. A person in Asia will experience less trouble and likely spend less on acquiring many of these mushrooms because they are popular and readily available.

When compared with the cost of other medications, especially current cancer treatments, mushrooms are significantly less expensive. Even those that are hard to source or considered expensive, do not compare to what we pay for chemotherapy, radiation, and other cancer-fighting drugs.

As outlined in this book, there is much evidence that mushrooms can benefit humans for a wide host of issues. The research around Lentinin (from Shiitakes) and PSK (from Turkey Tail), is especially profound. Their use in treating cancers and as an adjunct with chemotherapy is ground-breaking and could change the way we fight and treat the biggest killer of our times.

The importance of the research cannot be understated. Worldwide, 1 in 6 deaths is caused by cancer. The estimated cost, in 2010, of cancer worldwide was 1.16 trillion (USD). In 2018, 9.6 million deaths were attributed to cancer worldwide. Lung, colon, and prostate cancers were the top three leading to death. Lung, colon, and breast were the most common types of cancer afflicting people across the globe.[1]

CHAPTER 4

HEALING PROPERTIES OF MUSHROOMS

Mushrooms are neither a plant nor vegetable; they are class by themselves and form their own kingdom. To understand the healing possibilities of mushrooms, it is helpful to know what a mushroom is made up of and how it reproduces. In this book, there will be references to different parts of the mushroom as sometimes it is only one part of a mushroom that is being studied and/or has shown usefulness.

Mushroom Basics

Mushrooms are closer in relationship to animals, yet they resemble plants in their structures. They are made up of mycelium, usually a fruiting body, and spores, although there are exceptions. They can grow on the ground, on live trees, on dead trees, in sawdust, in compost, and by parasitizing insects. The kingdom is extremely complex, and current research is still only just touching the surface.

Mycelium

This is the vegetative body that is necessary for the fungi to grow. It is comparable to the root system of a plant. It consists of long white strands that look akin to webbing or threads. Mycelium is fixed to its host and spreads, often quite widely. Much of it is underground or beneath tree bark and not immediately visible to the forager. This varies widely by mushroom type, though. For some species, the mycelium is easy to locate or find, with a little digging or pulling back of the tree bark.

The mycelium must exist to produce the fruiting body, the physical mushroom, as we know it. It is a marker for where a mushroom is about to grow. Mushrooms will never grow in a place where they have not established a mycelium network.

Mycelium grows in places where spores (the mushroom "seeds") have established themselves. For the mycelium to produce a physical mushroom, two spores must meet, both produce mycelium and join together. Their joining signals the fruiting stage of the fungi.

There are some mushrooms that never or rarely move past the mycelium stage.

Fruiting Body

This is the manifestation of the mushroom. The image you see when you think of a mushroom, that is the fruiting body. They do not all look like a classic button mushroom, though. The fruiting bodies are quite diverse. The realm of mushroom bodies is a wild one, which sometimes seems not of this world.

Spores

Once a fruiting body matures, it produces spores, usually on the underside of the body. Spores are like the seeds of a plant. The spores drop, or the wind whisks them away, and if they land in favorable conditions, they will germinate. Each mushroom releases thousands of spores. The traveling spores are important because mushrooms are rooted in the ground, and have no other way of spreading. Reproduction depends on spores being released.

When the spores germinate, they produce mycelium. Two compatible spores must meet and create mycelium together in order to create a fruiting body. Once they create mycelium together, the cycle starts anew.

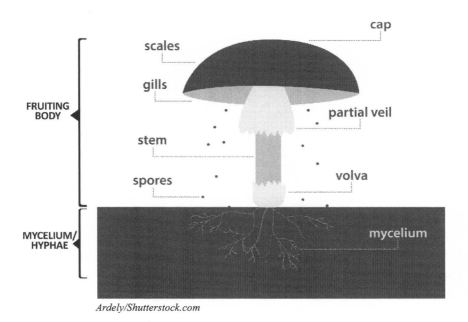

Ardely/Shutterstock.com

The majority of medicinal properties are found in the fruiting body. Tests being conducted often use the whole mushroom, as it holds the most potential usefulness. Other tests extract properties from the body and seclude them to determine the exact benefits provided. This is important to understand specifically which parts of the fungi have healing properties. The individual elements are easier to study and understand when isolated from the larger body. Additionally, by secluding the elements, it is possible to magnify the strengths and make a stronger medicine.

The difference has a great impact. A person may need to eat 6-8 ounces of a whole mushroom to receive the same medicinal dose as found in a concentrated formulated extract.

In medicinal preparations, the mycelium is sometimes used in combination with the fruiting body. The mycelium does not have the same properties as the body and has been shown to add value to the medicinal components of the fungi. This varies widely by mushroom type, though. Harvesting the mycelium is not always easy, especially when wild foraging. Also, harvesting the mycelium can harm the mushroom colony by preventing future growth.

Medicinal Properties

Research into all types and varieties of mushrooms show that they contain specific properties that have medical potential. Fungi are known to have antioxidants, boost immune health, decrease inflammation, combat cancer cells, boost brain activity, and positively enhance cognitive functioning.

Lion's Mane, for example, has demonstrated an ability to increase brain health through a naturally occurring peptide, called NGF (nerve growth factor). This is significant because it specifically is being tested for increasing the survival of neurons in the brain affected by neurodegenerative diseases, like Alzheimer's and dementia. With the current lack of successful treatments available to people suffering from these afflictions, mushrooms may play a very crucial role.

Chaga, Reishi, and Cordyceps, are all known to increase antioxidant activity. Antioxidants are responsible for fighting the free radicals that attack the body and accelerate the aging process. As we age, free radicals become more prominent in our body and quicken the deterioration of our minds and bodies. Improving the antioxidant levels in our bodies is a natural way to combat the signs of aging.

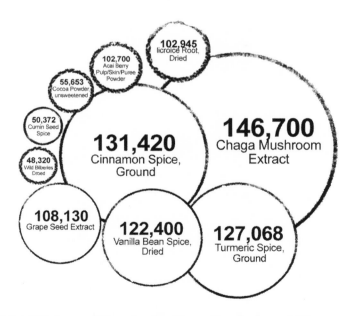

ORAC Values of Top Antioxidant Foods (per 100 grams)

In addition to increasing antioxidants that help fight the downsides of aging, many fungi demonstrate the ability to boost the immune system. This is important for aging populations since immunity is often decreased in older people. Immune systems wear down over time and are known to struggle at effectively combating diseases, even those like the flu, which it could, at one time, fight. There are also many immune-diminishing diseases that affect all ages, not just the elderly. Chaga, in particular, has shown significant effectiveness in promoting immune health. Shiitake also are proven to enhance the immune system, specifically with people fighting cancer.

Another medicinal use for mushrooms is to decrease inflammation. Specifically, they are being used to combat arthritis, including rheumatoid arthritis. Untreated inflammation significantly limits a person's ability to function. Lion's Mane, Chicken of the Woods, and Shiitake, to name just a few, are being studied for their effectiveness in decreasing, and potentially eliminating, inflammation.

Cancer-fighting drugs are big business worldwide, and their effectiveness varies widely. There are so many cancer types, it is difficult to understand all the properties and causes of them. Fungi are being investigated to treat all types of cancer, including breast, prostate, lung, and liver cancers. Each cancer is different and each medicinal mushroom treatment must be formulated for each specific one. Some mushrooms, like Reishi and Chaga, have demonstrated broader abilities for many types of cancers. While the fungi properties themselves have been verified, what still needs research is how they interact with the human body and the best way to benefit from them. This area

12

of study has burgeoned in the last 5-10 years as interest grows.

Fundamental Medicinal Properties of Mushrooms

Polysaccharides, specifically Beta-D-Glucan and Proteoglycans

Polysaccharides show potential in modulating the immune system. They increase immune response and adjust to the needs of the body. All mushrooms have some type of polysaccharide in them, though the type and amount varies widely.

Many plants have polysaccharides, although not as complex as mushrooms or with as many immunological possibilities.

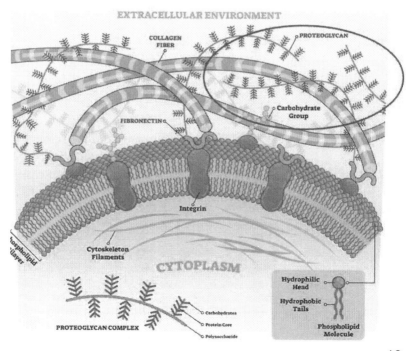

VectorMine/Shutterstock.com

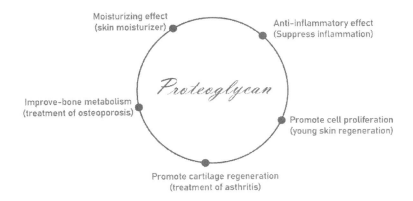

Proteins

All mushrooms have some amount of protein, and many are quite protein-rich. Besides the nutritional value, the proteins in several mushrooms have also shown potential in boosting the immune system.

Triterpenes (triterpenoids)

These are composed of terpenes, which are a diverse group of organic compounds. They are found naturally in plants, animals, and fungi. The uses are multiple and complicated, scientifically. The triterpene, squalene, found in shark liver oil, was a precursor to modern-day steroids.

Phenols

Naturally occurring chemical compounds, phenols are used in antiseptics, disinfectants, and fungicides.

Sterols

A subgroup of steroids, sterols occur naturally in animals, plants, and mushrooms. Cholesterol is a sterol. They are essential to cell membrane structure.

Statins

A statin is a drug that lowers cholesterol. They were first isolated from mushrooms, specifically Aspergillus fungi. Many mushrooms contain high levels of naturally occurring statins.

Mushrooms grow around the world, and even the same species may not possess the same bio-active properties. A 2015 study of polypores determined that location and growing medium impacted chemical composition.[2] This is extremely important when considering the medicinal properties of fungi and their potential healing. F.pinicola harvested in one region may not have the same bio-active elements as one grown in a neighboring region. While it seems the medicinal properties still exist in each one, it is the degree of efficacy that is in question.

For organizations researching best practices to grow medicinal mushrooms, this needs to be explored further. After all, the strain with the best medicinal properties is the one needed to treat diseases, and there needs to be testing to select for this. The growing medium also plays a role. Many mushrooms grow on a variety of mediums, for example, trees, rotted stumps, and sawdust. In mushroom growing operations, the growers generally select the grow medium based on ease of use and productivity. Whether the medium is the best growing type for medicinal use is often overlooked.[3]

Current known biologically active constituents in mushrooms:

- **Tolypocladium inflatum** – a source for the immunosuppressant cyclosporine, which is used for treating rheumatoid arthritis, Crohn's disease, and psoriasis. It is also used to stop rejection during organ transplants. This fungus also produces antiamoebin, which shows promise in treating malaria.

- **Almond mushroom** (Agaricus subrufescens) – a bio-active steroid was discovered and isolated from this mushroom

- **Cordyceps** (Ophiocordyceps sinensis) - used to create cordycepin, which treats abnormally fast heart rhythm. Cordycepin is now manufactured synthetically.

- **Devil's Tooth** (Hydnellum peckii) produces atromentin. Atromentin has been shown to kill isolated leukemia cells. It may also treat 'smooth muscle condition', which can be fatal in infants.

- **Shiitake** (Lentinula edodes) – a source for Lentinan and AHCC, which are currently being studied as a treatment for cancer.

- **Split Gill** (Schizophyllum commune) – the source for schizophyllan which stimulates the immune system and assists in drug delivery.

- **Turkey Tail** (Coriolus versicolor) – a protein-bound source of PSP (polysaccharide peptide) that has shown promise as an anti-tumor treatment. Additionally, PSK (polysaccharide krestin) which has been and still is being studied as a treatment for cancer. Additionally, a peptide isolated from Turkey Tail has shown promise in treating Type 2 diabetes by lowering blood sugar.

- **Reishi** (Ganoderma lucidum) – produces Ganoderic Acid, a triterpenoid, which is an anti-bacterial, anti-inflammatory, antiviral, anti-hypertension, and an antioxidant.

- **Aspergillus terreus** – this mold fungus was used in creating the first generation of statins, which are used to lower cholesterol.

Two Successful Applications of Medicinal Mushrooms

These studies are two of many that demonstrate the real-life effectiveness of mushrooms in treating medical conditions. While many studies are still being conducted, with exact results pending, these two are indisputable success stories. The majority of mushroom extracts are still in the trial phase and haven't gone through human testing. However, these two extracts have gone through clinical human trials and have shown fantastic results.

Case Study One: AHCC Extract for Boosting the Immune System

An extract from the Basidiomycete clade of mushrooms, which includes Shiitake, is being studied for its effects on the immune system. This extract, called AHCC (Active hexose correlated compound), improved the immune system of mice undergoing chemotherapy treatment. Specifically, it increased resistance to viral and bacterial infections. When used in treating colitis, it showed promising anti-inflammatory effects.

Human studies have been done on patients with hepatocellular carcinoma and cirrhosis. AHCC enhanced liver function in these patients, as well as elevated anti-tumor activity. In patients with advanced cancers, AHCC showed potential in treating adverse effects brought on by chemotherapy. On the other hand, it showed no results when used with patients with early-stage prostate cancer.

Side effects for AHCC include itching and diarrhea.

Conclusion: This extract, found naturally in Shiitake, as well as other mushrooms, can potentially treat cancer. It has far fewer side effects than most cancer-fighting drugs on the market today. Shiitake mushrooms are mass-cultivated and easy to source the world over, fresh, and extracted.

Case Study Two: PSK Extract for Treating Cancers

PSK (polysaccharide krestin, a protein-bound polysaccharide), a component of Coriolus versicolor (Turkey Tail), has been studied extensively for its efficacy in treating cancer. Research shows it works best in conjunction with chemotherapy.

A 1994 study in Japan studied gastric cancer patients who received surgery and were undergoing chemotherapy.[4] Those taking PSK lived longer and were less likely to have cancer come back. A larger study in 2007 of gastric cancer stomach surgery patients showed that patients taking PSK with chemotherapy treatments lived longer.[5]

Patients with stage 2 and stage 3 rectal cancer were given PSK in combination with chemotherapy and radiation treatments. The PSK increased cancer-killing cells.[6] Another study showed that patients with colon cancer given PSK lived longer and had decreased recurrences of cancer.[7]

PSK given to patients with lung cancer who were undergoing chemotherapy showed improved immune function, increased body weight, improved well-being, fewer tumor-related symptoms, and extended survival rates.[8]

There are no known risks or adverse side-effects experienced in all the clinical trials of PSK use.

PSK-based extracts are approved by the Japanese government as a cancer treatment to be used alongside chemotherapy, surgery, and radiation. It is a best-selling drug in Japan.

CHAPTER 5

OVERVIEW OF MEDICINAL MUSHROOMS

T he abundance of mushroom species and their uses is incredible. The majority of medicinal mushrooms have been used for centuries in Asian medicine practices and have only become popular in the west in the last few decades. The research for many of these species is based on hundreds (or thousands) of years of use by eastern practitioners and have only had a limited amount of western-style medicinal research conducted on them. Human-based scientific research is lacking, though increased interest has furthered studies, and more is being learned every year.

This section will walk you through the most common medicinal mushrooms, their uses, and how and where they grow. The list is arranged alphabetically by scientific name for ease of use. Under each listing, you'll see the common names listed, of which there are often many. Common names can vary within countries and are often regional, especially the more widespread varieties. It gets quite confusing at times! Compounding this confusion are changes to the scientific names as DNA analysis is done, and genetics prove that the mushroom belongs in a different class. In all cases, I have attempted to be as comprehensive as possible. However, it is quite likely some have been missed. With over 10,000 types of mushrooms in the world, it is difficult to catalog them all.

Agaricus arvensis
(Common Names: Horse Mushroom)

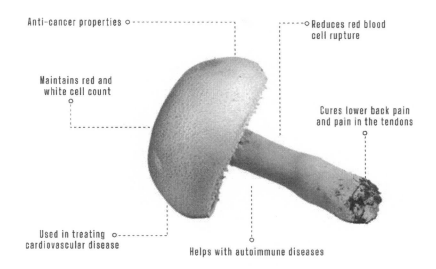

Anti-cancer properties

Reduces red blood cell rupture

Maintains red and white cell count

Cures lower back pain and pain in the tendons

Used in treating cardiovascular disease

Helps with autoimmune diseases

Milart/Shutterstock.com

Another well-known and widespread Agaricus type, the Horse Mushroom, potentially has a lot to offer. Current research is exploring its potential for maintaining red and white cell counts. Disorders with abnormal cell counts include cancer, cardiovascular disease, and immune diseases. It has also shown promise in animal studies to reduce red blood cell rupture.[9] In Chinese medicine, it is used as a treatment for cancer. It also has been stated to cure lower back pain and pain in the tendons.

The Horse Mushroom grows wild in North America, Europe, Australia, New Zealand, and West Asia. It is prized for its large size and delicious flavor. It is not grown commercially, although it can be propagated indoors.

Perhaps because it is so widespread and common, there is no demand for commercial supplies.

Main application: Cancer, Cardiovascular disease, Immune diseases, Lower Back Pain.

Agaricus bisporus

(Common Names: Crimini, Portobello, White Button, Baby Bella)

Improves gut bacteria health

Anti-cancer properties

High level of antioxidants

Antimicrobial agent

Improves age-related problems such as memory and cognitive function

Used in treating cardiovascular disease

Khumthong/Shutterstock.com

Chances are, you are quite familiar with this mushroom in all its forms. What most people don't know is that the white button mushroom is the same as the crimini mushroom, which is the same as the portobello mushroom, which is Agaricus bisporus. The differences in color and size relate to the strain and maturity of the mushroom. When it is young, it is small and either white or brown. As it matures, it turns all brown and increases in size. Small Agaricus bisporus always used to be brown until a farmer mycologist found a white one growing on his mushroom farm. He took the mutated version, developed it further, and introduced the white button mushroom to the world.

Besides being the most cultivated edible mushroom in the world and a great source of nutrition, Agaricus bisporus also shows promise as an antioxidant, anticancer, and antimicrobial agent. It may also be used in treating cardiovascular disease. A study using rats showed that daily intake of Agaricus bisporus could improve age-related problems like memory and cognitive function. There was also a recent study comparing a meat diet with one using Agaricus bisporus as the protein source. The results showed the mushroom diet increased short-chain fatty acids, which are vital to gut bacteria health.[10]

Wild versions of Agaricus bisporus grow in Europe and North America.

Main application: Cancer, Antioxidant, Antimicrobial, Cardiovascular disease, Age, Cognitive Function, Memory, Gut Health.

Agaricus campestris
(Common Names: Field Mushroom)

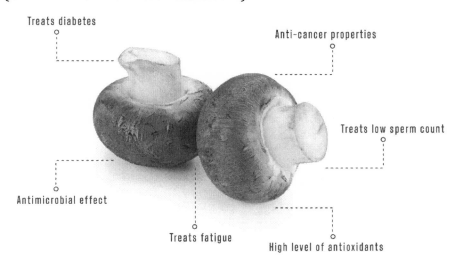

Treats diabetes

Anti-cancer properties

Antimicrobial effect

Treats low sperm count

Treats fatigue

High level of antioxidants

Hyrma/Elements.envato.com

A close relative of Agaricus bisporus, A. campestris is a well-known edible mushroom. It grows wild in lawns and meadows worldwide, and it looks much like its close cousin.

Field Mushroom studies reveal that it has the potential for treating diabetes because it increases the secretion of insulin. This mushroom also has anticancer, antimicrobial, and antioxidant properties. The field mushroom was recently tested for treating lung cancer and shows promise.[11] In Ayurvedic practices, Agaricus campestris is prescribed to treat fatigue and low sperm

Johannes Dag Mayer/Shutterstock.com

25

count. (Eaten whole, cooked, not powdered) The Field Mushroom is not commercially cultivated because it matures and deteriorates faster than is viable for commercial operators.

Main application: Diabetes, Cancer, Antimicrobial, Antioxidant, Lung Cancer, Fatigue.

Agaricus subrufescens, aka A. blazei, aka A. brasiliensis, aka A. rufotegulis.

(Common Names: Almond Mushroom, Himematsutake, Royal Sun Mushroom)

Picture Partners /Shutterstock.com

This well-known edible mushroom with a faint almond scent has been used in traditional and alternative medical practices for decades. Its main use is as a cancer-fighter. It is also prescribed for allergies, diabetes, dermatitis, hepatitis, and to fight infections. In animal studies, it has shown promise as an anti-tumor agent, and to have antiallergic, antidiabetic, and anti-infection properties. Additionally, it may contain anti-inflammatory properties and be useful in fighting inflammatory bowel diseases.

Specifically, human studies have shown that it improves insulin resistance for diabetics, reduces serum glucose, and lowers cholesterol levels.[12] It also reduces overall body fat.[13]

A study of cancer patients in remission showed that the Almond Mushroom improved quality of life; however, it did not extend life-expectancy.[14] It enhanced the activity of natural killer cells in gynecological cancer patients who were undergoing chemotherapy.[15]

A 2015 study in mice showed promise with this mushroom in treating malaria.[16] The antioxidant properties of Agaricus reduced parasites, reduced weight loss, and increased survival rates. The Almond Mushroom grows in North and South America as well as Europe and is cultivated extensively in Japan for its medicinal properties. This mushroom looks like a classic mushroom. It features a white or brown cap with brown gills underneath and a dense, stout stem. Agaricus mushroom is widely available fresh, freeze-dried, and in extracts, powders, teas, and compounds. There have been reports of toxic effects in the liver in some patients. A note about names and taxonomy: This mushroom has been through a lot of name changes, and it was thought for a long time that the species found on different continents were different varieties. Recently, through genetic testing, it has been shown that all four designations listed in the heading for this mushroom are the same mushroom. The name A. subrufescens is the oldest name and now encompasses all of them into one. In older research papers and guides, the name for this mushroom could be any of those four, but it all pertains to the same one. By far, the most common medicinal name for this mushroom is A. blazei.

Main application: Cancer, Allergies, Diabetes, Dermatitis, Hepatitis, Infections, Tumors, Allergies, Inflammation, IBS, High Cholesterol, Malaria, Antioxidant.

Auricularia Auricula-Judae

(Common Names: Jelly Ear Fungus, Kikurage, Wood Ear, Mu Ear, Jews Ear, Black Fungus)

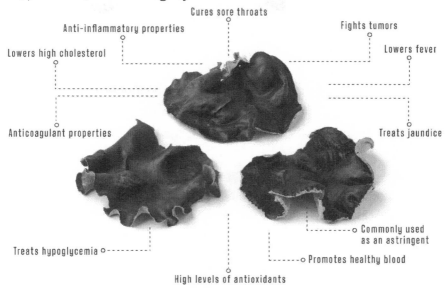

Cures sore throats

Anti-inflammatory properties

Fights tumors

Lowers high cholesterol

Lowers fever

Anticoagulant properties

Treats jaundice

Commonly used as an astringent

Treats hypoglycemia

Promotes healthy blood

High levels of antioxidants

Picture Partners/Shutterstock.com

This jelly fungus grows world-wide. Traditional medicinal uses include treatment for jaundice, sore throats, inflammation, and tired eyes. Gargling a broth made with the mushroom was recorded as a cure for a sore throat. It was also commonly used as an astringent. In China, it is consumed fresh in soups as a treatment for colds and fevers. And, in Ghana, it is used to promote healthy blood.

Recent studies have discovered Jelly Ear contains two glucans that may have tumor-fighting properties.[17] It has also shown promising results in treating

Vespa/Shutterstock.com

29

hypoglycemia and maintaining insulin and glucose levels.[18] A polysaccharide extracted from the Jelly Ear Fungus demonstrated anticoagulant properties.[19] Another study showed this fungus could reduce overall cholesterol levels, and specifically can lower bad cholesterol.[20] Also, Jelly Ear Fungus is shown to have antioxidant properties.[21] [22]

The Jelly Ear is edible, although not palatable to everyone due to its soft rubbery consistency. It is called jelly for a reason! Jelly Ear is a brown cup-shaped fungus that is gelatinous when it is young and becomes brittle and hard with age. There are often wrinkles or folds in the broad surface, which give it an even closer resemblance to an ear. Jelly Ear Fungus is cultivated commercially around the world.

Main application: Inflammation, Sore Throat, Fever, Jaundice, Astringent, Healthy Blood, Antioxidant, Tumor, Hypoglycemia, Anticoagulant, High Cholesterol.

Coriolus versicolor, aka Trametes versicolor, aka Polyporus versicolor.

(Common Names: Turkey Tail, Kawaratake, Yun Zhi.)

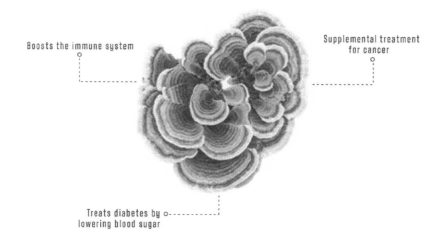

Boosts the immune system

Supplemental treatment for cancer

Treats diabetes by lowering blood sugar

Digoarpi/Shutterstock.com

This polypore mushroom is widespread around the world. Turkey Tail has been used in traditional Chinese medicine for centuries to boost the immune system and as a treatment for cancer. In Japan, an extract of Turkey Tail is an approved supplemental treatment for cancer, to go along with chemotherapy, surgery, and radiation, and it is a top-seller in the country. Studies in Japan showed increased life-expectancy after cancer when Turkey Tail was included with

Digoarpi/Shutterstock.com

31

treatment.[23] Western-style scientific studies exploring the use of Turkey Tail as a cancer-fighter are still being conducted, specifically for breast, prostate, liver, and stomach cancer.[24] [25] [26] [27]

It is also being studied for its potential use in treating Type 2 diabetes by lowering blood sugar.[28]

Turkey Tail grows on dead logs and stumps in overlapping layers. The caps are flat and average 8x5 cm and are 1-3 mm thick. The cap features different colored zones on top and white pores underneath. The multiple brown rings on the cap resemble a turkey's tail, hence the name.

This mushroom cannot be eaten fresh as it is leathery, tough, and unpalatable. Extracts, tinctures, powders, teas, and compounds are widely available.

Main application: Immune System, Cancer, Diabetes.

Flammulina velutipes

(Common Names: Enokitake, Enoki)

Treats cancer o--------

Adjusts the o--------
immune system

Antimicrobial o-------
properties

High levels o-------
of
antioxidants

--------o Fights signs of aging

--------o Anti-inflammatory

--------o Lowers high
cholesterol

--------o Treats
hypertension

Treats melanin-related issues

Treats neurodegenerative diseases

Picturepartners/Elements.envato.com

One of the four top-cultivated mushrooms because of its desirability as an edible; Enoki is also used as a medicinal in traditional eastern medicine. It is prescribed to treat cancer and adjust the immune system. Enoki also is used as an antimicrobial and antioxidant.

Current studies highlight Enoki's potential in treating neurodegenerative diseases, high cholesterol, inflammation, aging, melanin-related issues, and hypertension.[29]

The Enoki that is grown commercially is far different from the one found in the wild, aesthetically, at least. The genetics are the same, but because the commercial growing conditions are so

Pieter Bruin/Shutterstock.com

unique and different from Enoki in the wild, the results look nothing like the original.

As mentioned, Enoki is cultivated widely and can be found fresh, freeze-dried, powdered, and as extracts and tinctures.

Main Application: Cancer, Immune System, Antimicrobial, Antioxidant, Neurodegenerative diseases, High Cholesterol, Inflammation, Aging, Melanin Issues, Hypertension.

Fomitopsis betulina, formerly Piptoporus betulinus
(Common Names: Birch Polypore, Razer Strop)

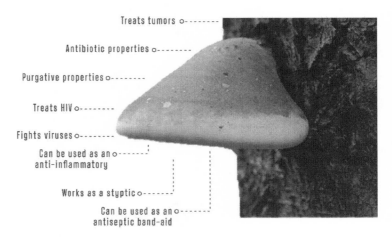

Treats tumors

Antibiotic properties

Purgative properties

Treats HIV

Fights viruses

Can be used as an anti-inflammatory

Works as a styptic

Can be used as an antiseptic band-aid

angel217/Shutterstock.com

Widely recognized for its medicinal properties, this is the polypore that was found in Otzi the Iceman's pouch. Speculation is that he carried it to treat whipworm since Birch Polypore is poisonous to that parasite. It could be carried for use as an antibiotic as well as a purgative.[30]

Birch Polypore has been used by cultures across the world as an anti-bacterial, anti-inflammatory, anti-parasitic, anti-viral, and styptic. Currently, birch polypore is being studied for cancer treatment. It contains properties that can inhibit new blood cell growth, which could be useful in treating tumors. It has been used in studies as an antiviral treatment against HIV with promising results.[31] Another interesting use of this polypore is as an anti-septic band-aid. The underside of the mushroom peels off when carefully cut and when wrapped around a laceration, it will stop the bleeding and protect the injury.

The birch polypore is a bracket fungus averaging 10-20 cm across. It grows exclusively on birch trees and is white when young, then changes to tan or gray as it ages. It grows commonly across Europe and North America, and it is not uncommon to see a birch tree covered with them. This mushroom is not commercially cultivated yet, although there have been promising developments recently. If you intend to wild-forage it, please do so responsibly. Birch polypore supplements are widely available as teas, tinctures, tonics, powders, and dried chunks.

Main application: Antibiotic, Purgative, Inflammation, Viruses, Styptic, Antiseptic, Cancer, HIV.

Fomitopsis officinalis

(Common Names: Agarikon)

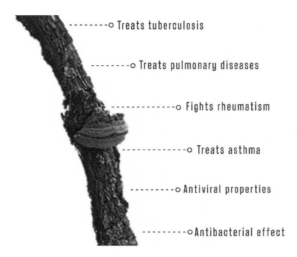

o Treats tuberculosis

o Treats pulmonary diseases

o Fights rheumatism

o Treats asthma

o Antiviral properties

o Antibacterial effect

shutterman007/Shutterstock.com

A great example of the complications in fungi species, until recently, the name Agarikon was applied interchangeably to both Fomitopsis officinalis and Laricifomes officinalis. In 2014, DNA analysis determined they are separate species. Research conducted on Agarikon, for this reason, is complicated as it is often difficult to determine which species is actually being studied. They are both wood-decay bracket fungi and look very much alike, which is the main reason for the confusion. The difference is which tree they grow on, which may or may not make a difference medicinally. Laricifomes officinalis grows on larch trees while Fomitopsis officinalis grows on Douglas fir, spruce, and hemlock. Information presented for this species includes both as if they are the same, since scientific research still lumps them together.

A bracket polypore mushroom, Agarikon has been used for

37

centuries to treat pulmonary diseases. In Mongolia, it is used to treat rheumatism and asthma. It is also prescribed traditionally as an antiviral and antibacterial. In Ancient Greece, it was used to treat tuberculosis. [32]

Agarikon produces Agaricin (agaric acid), which is an anti-inflammatory and parasympatholytic. Parasympatholytic agents reduce the activity of the parasympatholytic nervous system and can be used to treat overactive bladder, ulcers, IBS, and spasms.[33] Recent studies show Agarikon reduces inflammation and combats viral and bacterial infections. Uses being studied include treating bird flu, cowpox, swine flu, and the herpes virus.[34] [35]

Agarikon grows wild in Asia, Europe, and North America, although in Europe and Asia, it is almost extinct. It grows in old-growth forests, and habitat loss is the main reason it has all but disappeared in those areas. It is an enormous polypore, growing up to 60 cm long. It resembles a massive horse hoof and grows more each year it remains on the tree. When young, they are yellowish-white. As they decay, they turn mostly brown with concentric stripes of gray, white, and brown throughout.

Unrelated to human medicine but important nonetheless, the antimicrobial properties of Agarikon have shown promise in helping bees and colony collapse disorders. Tinctures, powders, and compounds of Agarikon can be found online. Because of its relative rarity, it is quite pricey.

Main application: Pulmonary diseases, Rheumatism, Asthma, Viruses, Antibacterial, Tuberculosis.

Fomitopsis pinicola

(Common Names: Red-Banded Polypore, Red-Belted Conk)

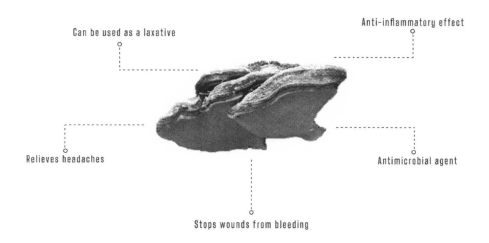

Can be used as a laxative

Anti-inflammatory effect

Relieves headaches

Antimicrobial agent

Stops wounds from bleeding

Tynza/Shutterstock.com

This conk variety of mushroom was used by native North American peoples to relieve headaches, to stop wounds from bleeding, as a laxative, and to induce vomiting. Traditional folk practitioners used it as an anti-inflammatory, anti-microbial, and styptic. In Europe, a drink made with F. pinicola was used to combat inflammation of the digestive tract. [36]

The Red-Banded Polypore is widely distributed across Asia, North America, and Europe. It grows on dying and dead conifer trees. When young, the cap is light brown with a white band around the edge. As it matures, the cap develops a deep rusty red color and keeps its white band for a while. The entire conk looks like it has been polished. It is tough, woody, and must be powdered or cooked into a tea or tincture to be consumed.

Despite being a common polypore, extracts of this mushroom are not common. There are sources for tinctures, teas, and powders available online or through a traditional medicine practitioner.

Main application: Headaches, Laxative, Inflammation, Antimicrobial, Styptic.

Ganoderma lucidum

(Common Names: Reishi, Lingzhi, Mannetake)

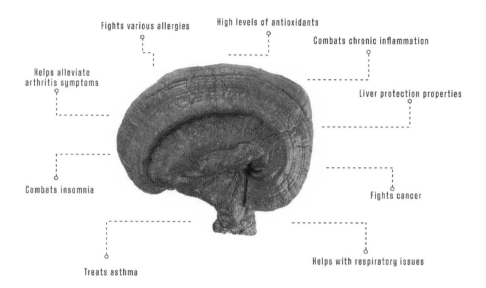

Fights various allergies

High levels of antioxidants

Combats chronic inflammation

Helps alleviate arthritis symptoms

Liver protection properties

Combats insomnia

Fights cancer

Treats asthma

Helps with respiratory issues

Stoonn/Elements.envato.com

This well-known healer has been used for centuries in Asia. It is prescribed regularly by holistic doctors to combat chronic inflammation, cancer, respiratory issues, asthma, insomnia, arthritis, and allergies. This medicinal mushroom has powerful anti-oxidant and liver-protection properties. In Japan, it is listed as an official treatment for cancer.[37]

Reishi is one of the most well-studied mushrooms, and its medicinal uses have been proven.[38] [39] [40] One important note: the majority of studies have been done on *Ganoderma*

James Aloysius Mahan V/Shutterstock.com

41

lucidum, the Asian variety of Reishi because it has been used medicinally for so long. The North American variety, *Ganoderma tsugae*, hasn't been studied as extensively; however, it is believed to have similar properties.

Reishi grows wild in Asia and North America. This polypore shelf mushroom starts orange and cream-colored and turns a deep, shiny red when it is fully mature. In Asia, *Ganoderma lucidum* grows on oak and maple trees. In North America, *Ganoderma tsugae* grows on hemlock trees. Reishi mushrooms are solid, fan-shaped shelves that grow individually on the tree. The shelf cap can get quite large, ranging from 5-30 cm wide and 1-4 cm thick.

Reishi can be cultivated, although the cultivated results are thought to be less pure than wild-foraged. The use of pesticides in grow operations has an effect on the pureness as well as the lack of natural, potentially important, growing conditions. Mushroom mycelium absorbs nutrients from its host, and there may be vital differences between growing wild on trees as opposed to man-made

sawdust blocks. Reishi extracts, powders,

tarapong srichaiyos/Shutterstock

tinctures, and drinks are widely available in health food stores, online, and through traditional Chinese medicine practitioners.

Main application: Inflammation, Cancer, Respiratory issues, Asthma, Insomnia, Arthritis, Allergies, Antioxidant, Liver protection.

Grifola frondosa
(Common Names: Maitake, Hen of the Woods, Hui Shu Hua)

Reduces tumors growth

Inhibits division and growth of cancer cells

Controls blood sugar levels in Type 2 diabetes

akepong srichaichana/Shutterstock.com

Shown to inhibit the division and growth of cancer cells[41] [42] [43], Maitake, also commonly called Hen of the Woods, is a medicinal powerhouse. It is also quite a tasty treat when used in culinary creations. Maitake is used primarily for cancers that affect the digestive and reproductive organs. This mushroom has also shown promise in controlling blood sugar levels in Type 2 diabetes when used regularly.[44] There has also been interesting research suggesting the use of Maitake to reduce tumor growth.[45]

Maitake grows primarily at the base of oak trees in eastern North America, China, and Japan. This polypore mushroom starts as a small fruiting body, about the size of a potato, and when mature reaches up to 2-7 cm across. They grow especially big in Japan, often reaching 45 kg. It is known as the "king of mushrooms" there with good reason! Maitake mushrooms grow multitudes of overlapping grayish-brown fronds, which give it the appearance of a hen sitting in the woods, hence the common name.

Maitake is cultivated widely, making it an easy mushroom to access fresh or dried.

Main application: Cancer, Diabetes, Tumors.

Hericium erinaceus

(Common Names: Lion's Mane, Monkey Head Mushroom, Mountain Monk Mushroom, Yamabushitake, Hou Tou Gu)

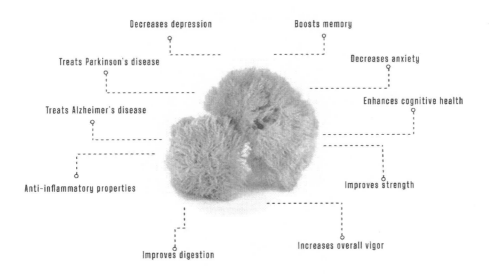

Decreases depression

Boosts memory

Treats Parkinson's disease

Decreases anxiety

Treats Alzheimer's disease

Enhances cognitive health

Anti-inflammatory properties

Improves strength

Improves digestion

Increases overall vigor

Phongsakon/Shutterstock.com

A stunning cream-white tooth mushroom with long, relaxed spines hanging off its often very large base, Lion's Mane earns its name. It is a sought-after edible and medicinal mushroom. Lion's Mane is the most clinically studied of all the mushroom types. Specifically, it has been examined for neurohealth properties.

Traditional Chinese medicine uses Lion's Mane to boost memory, enhance cognitive function, and improve concentration. It is also used to promote internal organ health (kidney, heart, liver, lung, and spleen). Eastern practitioners prescribe it for strength, overall vigor, and to improve digestion. It is also noted for its anti-inflammatory properties and is being looked into for treating Alzheimer's and Parkinson's diseases.

Clinical studies show that Lion's Mane improved cognitive function in a group of elderly Japanese men and women. Another study showed it decreased depression and anxiety in menopausal women.[46] [47]

Native to Europe, Asia, and North American, it grows in late summer to early fall. It is on the Red List of Endangered Species in 13 European countries due to habitat destruction and specificity of growing conditions. If you live in Europe, please check the status in your country before wild foraging this mushroom! Luckily, Lion's Mane is widely commercially cultivated and is available from specialty growers and online sources. It can be purchased fresh, dried, as a tincture, and as a tea.

Main application: Memory, Cognitive Health, Strength, Vigor, Digestion, Inflammation, Alzheimer's, Parkinson's, Depression, Anxiety.

Hericium sp.

There are other Hericium species that are often clumped with Lion's Mane because they are so similar in general appearance and taste. H. abietis, H. americanum, and H. coralloides are thought to have similar compounds to H. erinaceus. However, no studies have been done on these.

Hydnellum peckii

(Common Names: Devil's Tooth)

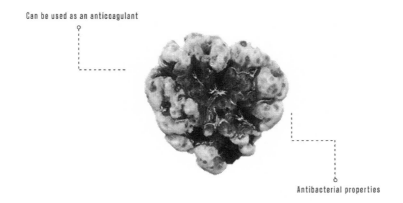

Can be used as an anticoagulant

Antibacterial properties

Henri Koskinen /Shutterstock.com

A completely bizarre and rather gross-looking fungus, Devil's Tooth is proof that not everything is how it looks. It exudes red drops like it is bleeding, and it is these deep red droplets that contain the medicinal properties.

There is a pigment in the droplets that is an anticoagulant called atromentin. Atromentin is also found in Agricales clade mushrooms and is also a known antibacterial. Research shows the atromentin in Devil's Tooth performs similarly to the well-known anticoagulant, heparin.[48]

Devil's Tooth grows in Europe, North America, Iran, Korea, and Australia. The fruiting body is off-white when young, and it forms into a dense cap with small teeth instead of gills. As it

47

ages, it turns into an unremarkable brown lump. It is not an edible fungus. This fungus is not available commercially. It is included in this list to demonstrate the widespread potential of mushrooms.

Main application: Anticoagulant, Antibacterial.

Inonotuus obliquus

(Common Names: Chaga, Kabanoanatake, Bai Hua Rong, Hua Jie Kong Jun, Cinder Conk)

Treats tumors topically

Combats cancer

Treats wounds

Treats Hepatitis C

Reduces swelling

Treats HIV

Lowers blood sugar levels in diabetics

Anti-hypoglycemic agent

Antioxidant properties

Works as an anti-microbial

Food Impressions /Shutterstock.com

In the bizarre world of fungi, Chaga is an odd-looking star. It grows out of the side of trees and looks like a large, protruding charred burl. In fact, burls are often mistaken for Chaga among new foragers. It can be found almost exclusively growing on birch trees, and traditional healers say that Chaga growing on any other type of tree does not have the same medicinal properties.

Chaga has been used for centuries to combat cancer, specifically cervical, breast, gastrointestinal, and lung cancer. It is used topically to treat tumors, wounds, and swelling. Recent research shows it can lower blood sugar. Russian scientific studies reveal Chaga has antioxidant properties and is gene-protective, meaning it works as an anti-microbial, anti-cancer, and anti-hypoglycemic agent. It has also shown success in treating HIV and Hepatitis C. To many, Chaga is the wonder-mushroom that boosts the immune system and fights off free-radicals to reduce signs of aging.[49] [50] Not technically a mushroom, though often referred to as one, Chaga is instead a giant ball of mycelium, which is like the seed of a mushroom. Because birch trees are widespread around the world, so too is Chaga. It grows on living birch trees in cold climates. There is no commercial cultivation of Chaga. The market for Chaga is large worldwide, and it is easily found online or in health-food stores in powder, tincture, or tea form. The benefits of Chaga seem to vary based on when it is harvested and where, with Siberian Chaga potentially having higher concentrations of healing properties, although this isn't conclusive. To get the full medicinal benefit, Chaga needs to be heated. The heat extracts the nutrients, so they become bio-available to the human body.

Main application: Cancer, Tumors, Wounds, Swelling, Diabetes, Antioxidant, Antimicrobial, Hypoglycemia, HIV, Hepatitis C.

Laetiporus sulphureus

(Common Names: Chicken of the Woods, Sulphur Shelf, Chicken Fungus)

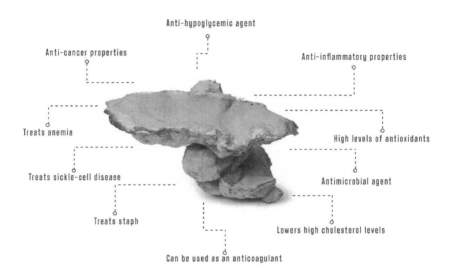

Anti-hypoglycemic agent

Anti-cancer properties

Anti-inflammatory properties

Treats anemia

High levels of antioxidants

Treats sickle-cell disease

Antimicrobial agent

Treats staph

Lowers high cholesterol levels

Can be used as an anticoagulant

Picturepartners/Elements.envato.com

With its unmistakable bright orange overlapping dense shelves, Chicken of the Woods is a prized find among mushroom foragers. It is the dense meatiness of the body that people seek out and where it gets its name. Chicken of the Woods, however, also has some strong medicinal properties.

Chicken of the Woods has been shown to have anticancer, antimicrobial, hypoglycemic, anti-inflammatory, and anti-oxidant properties. Studies

Tunatura/Shutterstock.com

have shown it can reduce cholesterol and potentially has anti-coagulant abilities. Chicken of the Woods also produces a lectin (LSL) that may be useful in treating Staph, Sickle-cell disease, and anemia.[51]

Although there have been numerous attempts, the commercial cultivation of Chicken of the Woods is not possible yet. It can be grown at home through inoculated plugs, but it is time-intensive, and results are varied. Powders, tinctures, and extracts are difficult to find.

Main application: Cancer, Hypoglycemia, Inflammation, Antioxidant, Antimicrobial, High Cholesterol, Anticoagulant, Staph, Sickle-cell, Anemia.

Laetiporus sp.

Within the Laetiporus clade, there are 18 types. They are region and often tree specific, which makes a scientific study interesting when attempting to make broad statements about the values of this mushroom. Each type needs to be evaluated individually to be certain of its medicinal qualities.

L. sulphureus grows throughout the eastern United States, Canada, and Europe. L. gilbertsonii and L. conifericola grow in the western United States, L. montanus grows in central Europe and China, L. persincinus grows in Africa, Asia, Australia, and North and South America. This mushroom type is widespread, yet the biology is sometimes unique between types.

Laricifomes officinalis, see Fomitopsis officinalis.

Lentinula edodes
(Common Names: Shiitake, Xiang Gu, Fragrant Mushroom)

Works as an anti-microbial

Reduces high cholesterol levels

Slows tumors growth

Fights cancer cells

Enhances the immune system

Digitalr/Elements.envato.com

A popular culinary mushroom around the world, Shiitake is also a widely used medicinal fungus. It has been shown to reduce cholesterol levels[52] and to work as an anti-microbial.[53] There is ongoing research into the ability of Shiitake to enhance the immune system[54] and slow tumor growth.[55] The shiitake mushroom grows on dying and decaying deciduous trees, like oak, maple, chestnut, poplar, chestnut, and ironwood. It is native to East Asia and has been cultivated since 1209 in China. In Asia, where it is extremely popular for eating and medicinal use, cultivated varieties are widespread. But it wasn't until the 1980s that other countries began growing it as well. Currently, it is now cultivated around the world and makes up around 25% of the total world production of mushrooms.

Shiitake mushrooms have light to dark brown caps with white

gills and grow individually or in small groups. The caps range from 10-20 cm in diameter and are curled at the edges, a distinguishing characteristic. Being the 2nd most popular mushroom in the world, Shiitakes are easily found fresh and dried and in tinctures, teas, compounds, and powders.

Main application: High Cholesterol, Antimicrobial, Tumor, Immune System, Cancer.

Lignosus rhinocerus

(Common Names: Tiger's Milk)

Malaysia's national treasure, this polypore mushroom has been used for centuries as traditional medicine. Indigenous peoples used Tiger's Milk as a general tonic and to treat fever, itching, asthma, coughs, cancer, food poisoning, swollen breasts, and to heal wounds. Current studies are researching its efficacy for nerve regeneration and as a treatment for neurodegenerative diseases.[56] [57]

Found only in tropical rainforests in Asia, Tiger's Milk has always been rare and is treasured when found. This mushroom grows solitarily from an underground mycelium reserve, called the sclerotium, which looks like a dense tuber. The stem is long and culminates on top into a wide, flat, brown cap. The mushroom is harvested with the fruiting body and the sclerotium, which holds the medicinal powers. Because the entire body is harvested, it cannot grow back, and this has led to its increasingly rare and endangered status.

Fortunately, in 2008, a Malaysian researcher, Tan Chon Seng, discovered how to cultivate it, and now it can be grown commercially. This new success in cultivating Tiger's Milk has cleared the path for new studies and determinations as to its medicinal value. Currently, Tiger's Milk mushroom can be difficult and expensive to source outside of Malaysia. Hopefully, that will change soon as the cultivation process is refined, and as research continues.

Main application: Nerve Regeneration, Neurodegenerative diseases, Fever, Itching, Asthma, Cancer.

Ophiocordyceps sinensis, formerly Cordyceps sinensis (Common Names: Cordyceps, Caterpillar fungus, Chinese caterpillar fungus, Dong Chong Xia Cao, Semitake, Hsia ts'ao tung ch'ung, Yarsha gumba, Tochukas)

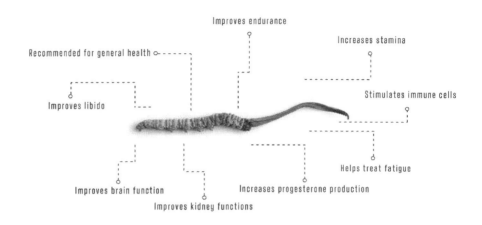

Improves endurance

Increases stamina

Recommended for general health

Stimulates immune cells

Improves libido

Helps treat fatigue

Improves brain function

Increases progesterone production

Improves kidney functions

PattyPhoto/Shutterstock.com

Mushrooms don't get much weirder than the cordyceps, it is truly a bizarre species. If you've ever wondered if aliens are real, take a moment to study this mushroom. This fungus parasitizes caterpillar and insect larvae and proceeds to consume the insect nutrients as it grows. It goes a bit beyond that, though, because the fungi also forces the zombified bodies of the insect to move to better growing locations for the Cordyceps.

Jiangdi/Shutterstock.com

56

After the cordyceps takes over the larvae host, it grows groups of brown or orange finger-like spindles out of the corpse. The spindly fingers are 2-3 cm long and are slightly bulbous at the tip. The historical classification of cordyceps includes the fungus and the insect body as one thing since they are inseparable.

In Chinese medicine, Cordyceps is recommended for all illnesses and is thought to be a general-use tonic. It is claimed to improve endurance, stamina, libido, appetite, and to increase longevity. In non-human trials, cordyceps has been shown to stimulate immune cells, increase progesterone production, and improve kidney function.[58] Cordyceps studies also found that it can help treat fatigue and improve brain function.[59] [60]

Native to the Himalayan Mountains, Cordyceps recently became cultivated around the world, mainly for medicinal uses. The cultivation process is still being tested and perfected, as people learn how best to stimulate the fungi. Cultivated varieties use just the mycelium or grow it on rice or barley grains. They do not parasitize insects. Cultivators say this produces a better quality cordyceps, while purists insist it is not real cordyceps without the parasitic element.

The demand for cordyceps has greatly increased in recent years as the benefits have become more well-known, and folks seek sources. It can be quite expensive; this is especially true of wild-foraged cordyceps, which have been over-harvested and exploited. A kilogram of low-quality wild-foraged Tibetan cordyceps sold for $3,000 US in 2007.

Main application: General Health, Endurance, Stamina, Immune issues, Fatigue, Progesterone, Kidney Function, Brain Function, Libido.

Panellus Stipticus

(Common Names: Bitter Oyster Mushroom)

Stops hemorrhaging

Can be used as a purgative

Jolanda Aalbers/Shutterstock.com

A common mushroom found wild in Australia, Asia, Europe, and North America, the Bitter Oyster doesn't taste good, but it has medicinal properties. In Chinese medicine, it is used as a purgative and to stop hemorrhaging. Current research mainly focuses on the unique bioluminescence of this fungus as opposed to medical uses.

The Bitter Oyster mushroom is found in Europe, Australia, New Zealand, North America, and parts of Asia. It grows in overlapping bunches and resembles the common Oyster mushroom (P. ostreatus) except significantly smaller and with a slightly fuzzy cap.

Main application: Hemorrhaging.

Phellinus linteus
(Common Names: Black Hoof Mushroom, Meshimakobu, Mesima, Sang Huang)

Alleviates menstruation problems

Cancer-fighting effects

Treats gastrointestinal issues

Treats myocardial ischemia-reperfusion

High levels of antioxidants

Anti-inflammatory properties

Is beneficial for diabetics

Fights viruses

Antimicrobial agent

Nadia Yong/Shutterstock.com

For centuries, Black Hoof Mushroom has been used in traditional Asian medicinal practices to treat cancer, gastrointestinal issues, menstrual issues, and hemorrhaging. The earliest mention of its use is from 2000 years ago during the Han dynasty. Harvard Medical School has studied the cancer-fighting effects of the Black Hoof Mushroom and reports that it shows promise.[61] However, more research is needed to determine the exact benefits. It was also studied as a treatment for breast cancer with promising results. Other cancers it may help include colon, lung, liver, oral, skin, and prostate.[62] [63]A study of people with pancreatic cancer showed it improved overall outcomes when combined with chemotherapy and/or radiation.[64]

Black Hoof Mushroom is shown to produce antioxidants as well as being an inhibitor of glycation, which is a biomarker for diabetes. Modern studies demonstrate Black Hoof Mushroom to be antimicrobial, antiviral, antioxidative, anti-inflammatory, and immunomodulatory.[65] It has also been studied for and showed good results in treating myocardial ischemia-reperfusion (IR), which is a bruising of the tissues related to cardiac arrest and surgery, chronic wounds, and diabetic foot ulcers.[66] This aptly named hoof-shaped mushroom grows wild in Asia. It is dark brown or black and is found on mulberry trees. Extracts, powders, teas, and tinctures are widely available online, in health-food stores, and from traditional medicine practitioners.

Main application: Cancer, Menstruation Issues, Gastrointestinal Issues, Antioxidant, Diabetes, Antimicrobial, Viruses, Inflammation, Myocardial Ischemia-Reperfusion.

Pleurotus cornucopiae

(Common Names: Horn of Plenty, Branched Oyster Mushroom, Tamogi-Take Mushroom)

Treats high blood pressure

Richsouthwales/Shutterstock.com

An Oyster mushroom type that grows wild across Europe, Mexico, and the United States, this one looks somewhat similar to the popular P. ostreatus but with a long, thick stem that gives it the "horn of plenty" name. It is grown commercially in Asia on a small scale.

Research studies show promise with P. cornucopiae treating high blood pressure.[67]

Main application: High Blood Pressure.

Pleurotus cystidiosus, P. abalonus

(Common Names:, Maple Oyster)

Treats diabetes o- - - - - - - - - - -

Kaiskynet Studio/Shutterstock.com

A type of Oyster mushroom found on maple trees; it looks nearly identical to P. ostreatus. It is often difficult to differentiate between the different oyster species, especially in the wild. New types are still being discovered as DNA analysis becomes more common. This species is commercially cultivated in Taiwan and Thailand as a food and medicine. Research indicates it has potential in treating diabetes.[68]

Main application: Diabetes.

Poungsaed-Studio/Shutterstock.com

Pleurotus ostreatus

(Common Names: Oyster Mushroom, Hirataki, Ping Gu)
below image: King Oyster Mushroom

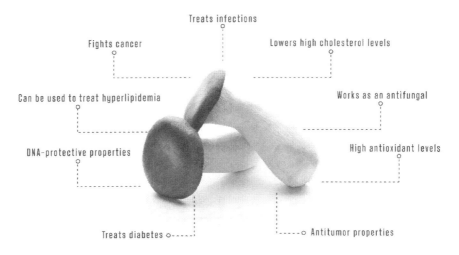

Treats infections

Fights cancer

Lowers high cholesterol levels

Can be used to treat hyperlipidemia

Works as an antifungal

DNA-protective properties

High antioxidant levels

Treats diabetes

Antitumor properties

GitaKulinica/Elements.envato.com

Widely cultivated around the world as an edible, Oyster mushrooms are gaining popularity as a medicine, as well. This species of Oyster mushroom, P. ostreatus, is the most commonly cultivated and widely studied.

In traditional cultures, Oyster mushrooms are used for diabetes treatment, hyperlipidemia, fighting cancer, and treating infections. Current in vitro studies show it working as an antifungal, antitumor, and lipid-lowering agent (cholesterol). There are also preliminary studies showing its efficacy as an antioxidant and anti-aging treatment.[69]

Oyster mushrooms grow in overlapping clumps on the trunks of dead or dying deciduous trees. They have minimal to no stem, and their cap is broad and fan-shaped, resembling that of

64

the bivalve oyster. The caps are generally whitish-gray but can also be tan or brown.

The oyster mushroom, while widely known as being a gourmet edible, is only just finding its way into medical research. Oyster mushrooms can be eaten fresh, although it is unknown if the medicinal benefits are the same in fresh vs. dried types.

Main application: Diabetes, Hyperlipidemia, Cancer, Infections, High Cholesterol, Fungal Diseases, Tumors, Antioxidant, Anti-aging.

Pleurotus tuber-regium

A tropical species of Oyster mushroom, this type is found in Africa, Asia, Australia, and New Zealand. It is genetically and biologically distinct from other Oyster mushrooms and cannot cross-breed.

As P. tuber-regium grows, it consumes dead wood and stores the nutrients in a sclerotium (a hard tuber-like storage sack) underground. Both the fruiting body and the sclerotium are choice edibles.

The sclerotium and mushroom are both used in traditional medicinal practices to treat headaches, colds, fevers, stomach ailments, asthma, high blood pressure, and smallpox.[70] Current studies show P. tuber-regium possesses antiviral properties[71] and demonstrates promise in treating diabetes.[72]

Commercial cultivation is not common with this species of Oyster mushroom. However, it may happen soon.

Main application: Cold, Fever.

Taiwanofungus camphoratus

(Common Names: Stout Camphor Fungus)

In Taiwan, where this mushroom is endemic, Stout Camphor Fungus is used as a medicine to treat cancer, itching, allergies, and fatigue, as well as protecting the liver. Recent studies show this mushroom to have anticancer and antioxidant properties as well as an anti-mutagenic ability and DNA-protective properties.

A 2016 study investigating the use of Stout Camphor Fungus for diabetics found it has potential as it affects glucose-induced insulin secretion. Stout Camphor Fungus also contains a polysaccharide that may have anti-HBV (hepatitis B) properties.[73 74]

This fungus only grows wild in Taiwan and only on the camphor tree. Because of its medicinal properties, it has been over harvested. Wild versions can be quite expensive. Thankfully, though, commercial cultivation methods have been developed, and now the fungus can be grown on farms.

Main application: Cancer, Allergies, Fatigue, Liver Issues, Antioxidant, Diabetes, Hepatitis B.

Tolypocladium inflatum

This complicated fungus has given the medical and specifically pharmaceutical world a lot. T. inflatum is the poster child of the potential of mushrooms and their medicinal properties. T. inflatum is a mold, discovered in a 1969 soil sample in Norway. Researchers found that under specific conditions, the fungi mold produced an immunosuppressant. This immunosuppressant was named Cyclosporine A. Cyclosporine A is used to manage autoimmune diseases as well as to prevent rejection in organ transplants. Cyclosporine A-based medicines are currently produced by the pharmaceutical company, Novartis, and they are a huge revenue-generator for them.

In addition to being an immunosuppressant, Cyclosporine A is also used to treat inflammation, fungal infections, skin diseases (like psoriasis and eczema), Crohn's disease, and parasite infections. Any medical concern that involves the immune system has the potential for being treated with cyclosporine. It is being tested as a treatment for Type 1 diabetes, rheumatoid arthritis, and HIV-1.[75] Cyclosporine A based medicines are only available as prescribed by a doctor. There are potential long-term side effects, which include reduced kidney function and increased blood pressure.

ciclosporin

StudioMolekuul/Shutterstock.com

Main application: Immunosuppressant, Inflammation, Fungal Diseases, Psoriasis, Eczema, Crohn's Disease, Diabetes, Rheumatoid Arthritis, HIV-1.

Tricholoma matsutake

(Common Names: Matsutake)

Antimicrobial properties

Anti-inflammatory effects

Motghnit/Elements.envato.com

A highly prized and expensive mushroom, T. matsutake is sought out for its unique and pungent umami-aromatic odor and flavor. Matsutake is also known to have antimicrobial and anti-inflammatory properties.[76]

Matsutake grows wild in Asia, Europe, and North America in association with pine trees. They are not commercially cultivated. Due to the demand and inability to be commercially grown, matsutake foraging is lucrative as well as potentially very damaging to the ecosystem as the interest is about making money instead of preserving or conserving the environment in which they grow.

Main application: Antimicrobial, Anti-inflammatory.

68

Medicinal Mushrooms Arranged Alphabetically by Latin Name, with English Name and Common Uses

LATIN NAME	COMMON ENGLISH NAME	USES
Agaricus arvensis	Horse Mushroom	Cancer, Cardiovascular disease, Immune diseases, Lower Back Pain
Agaricus bisporus	Button Mushroom, Portobello	Cancer, Antioxidant, Antimicrobial, Cardiovascular disease, Age, Cognitive Function, Memory, Gut Health
Agaricus campestris	Field Mushroom	Diabetes, Cancer, Antimicrobial, Antioxidant, Lung Cancer, Fatigue
Agaricus subrufescens (aka Agaricus blazei, Agaricus brasiliensis, Agaricus rufotegulis)	Almond Mushroom	Cancer, Allergies, Diabetes, Dermatitis, Hepatitis, Infections, Tumors, Allergies, Inflammation, IBS, High Cholesterol, Malaria, Antioxidant
Auricularia auricula-judae	Jelly Ear Fungus	Inflammation, Sore Throat, Fever, Jaundice, Astringent, Healthy Blood, Antioxidant, Tumor, Hypoglycemia, Anticoagulant, High Cholesterol
Coriolus versicolor (aka Trametes versicolor, Polyporus versicolor)	Turkey Tail	Immune System, Cancer, Diabetes

Flammulina velutipes	Enokitake, Enoki	Cancer, Immune System, Antimicrobial, Antioxidant, Neurodegenerative diseases, High Cholesterol, Inflammation, Aging, Melanin Issues, Hypertension
Fomitopsis betulina (aka Piptoporus betulinus)	Birch Polypore	Antibiotic, Purgative, Inflammation, Viruses, Styptic, Antiseptic, Cancer, HIV
Fomitopsis officinalis (aka Laricifomes officinalis)	Agarikon	Pulmonary diseases, Rheumatism, Asthma, Viruses, Antibacterial, Tuberculosis
Fomitopsis pincola	Red-Banded Polypore	Headaches, Laxative, Inflammation, Antimicrobial, Styptic
Ganoderma lucidum	Reishi	Inflammation, Cancer, Respiratory issues, Asthma, Insomnia, Arthritis, Allergies, Antioxidant, Liver protection,
Grifola Frondosa	Maitake, Hen of the Woods	Cancer, Diabetes, Tumors
Hericium erinaceus	Lion's Mane	Memory, Cognitive Health, Strength, Vigor, Digestion, Inflammation, Alzheimer's, Parkinson's, Depression, Anxiety
Hericium sp.	Coral Tooth etc	Same as H.erinaceus
Hydnellum peckii [not available commercially]	Devil's Tooth	Anticoagulant, Antibacterial

Inonotuus obliquus	Chaga	Cancer, Tumors, Wounds, Swelling, Diabetes, Antioxidant, Antimicrobial, Hypoglycemia, HIV, Hepatitis C
Laetiporus sulphureus	Chicken of the Woods	Cancer, Hypoglycemia, Inflammation, Antioxidant, Antimicrobial, High Cholesterol, Anticoagulant, Staph, Sickle-cell, Anemia
Laetiporus sp	Chicken of the Woods	Same as above
Lentinula edodes	Shiitake	High Cholesterol, Antimicrobial, Tumor, Immune System, Cancer
Lignosus rhinocerus	Tiger's Milk	Nerve Regeneration, Neurodegenerative diseases, Fever, Itching, Asthma, Cancer
Ophiocordyceps sinensis (aka Cordyceps sisnensis)	Cordyceps	General Health, Endurance, Stamina, Immune issues, Fatigue, Progesterone, Kidney Function, Brain Function, Libido
Panellus stipticus	Bitter Oyster Mushroom	Hemorrhaging
Phellinus linteus	Black Hoof Mushroom	Cancer, Menstruation Issues, Gastrointestinal Issues, Antioxidant, Diabetes, Antimicrobial, Viruses, Inflammation, Myocardial Ischemia-Reperfusion

Pleurotus ostreatus	Oyster Mushroom	Diabetes, Hyperlipidemia, Cancer, Infections, High Cholesterol, Fungal Diseases, Tumors, Antioxidant, Anti-aging
Pleurotus cornucopiae	Horn of Plenty	High Blood Pressure
Pleurotus cystidiosus	Abalone	Diabetes
Pleurotus tuber-regium	N/a	Cold, Fever
Taiwanofungus camphoratus (Antrodia camphorata)	Stout Camphor Fungus	Cancer, Allergies, Fatigue, Liver Issues, Antioxidant, Diabetes, Hepatitis B
Tolypocladium inflatum [not available commercially]	N/a	Immunosuppressant, Inflammation, Fungal Diseases, Psoriasis, Eczema, Crohn's Disease, Diabetes, Rheumatoid Arthritis, HIV-1
Tricholoma matsutake	Matsutake	Antimicrobial, Anti-inflammatory

CHAPTER 6

MEDICINAL MUSHROOMS ORGANIZED BY AILMENT

AILMENT	MEDICINAL MUSHROOMS
Aging	Flammulina velutipes, Pleurotus ostreatus
Allergies	Agaricus subrufescens, Ganoderma lucidum, Pleurotus ostreatus, Taiwanofungus camphoratus
Alzheimer's	Hericium erinaceus
Antibacterial	Fomitopsis betulina
Antibiotic	Fomitopsis betulina
Anticoagulant	Auricularia auricula-judae, Geastrum Fimbriatum, Hydnellum peckii, Laetiporus sulphureus, Lignosus rhinocerus
Antimicrobial	Agaricus bisporus, Agaricus campestris, Flammulina velutipes, Fomitopsis officinalis, Fomitopsis pincola, Inonotuus obliquus, Laetiporus sulphureus, Lentinula edodes, Phellinus linteus, Pleurotus ostreatus
Antioxidant	Agaricus subrufescens, Agaricus bisporus, Agaricus campestris, Auricularia auricula-judae, Flammulina velutipes, Ganoderma lucidum, Inonotuus obliquus, Laetiporus sulphureus, Ophiocordyceps sinensis, Phellinus linteus, Pleurotus ostreatus, Taiwanofungus camphoratus
Anxiety	Hericium erinaceus
Arthritis	Ganoderma lucidum

Asthma	Fomitopsis officinalis, Ganoderma lucidum, Lignosus rhinocerus
Brain Function	Ophiocordyceps sinensis
Cancer*	Agaricus subrufescens, Agaricus bisporus, Agaricus campestris, Coriolus versicolor, Flammulina velutipes, Fomitopsis betulina, Fomitopsis pincola, Ganoderma lucidum, Grifola frondosa, Inonotuus obliquus, Laetiporus sulphureus, Lentinula edodes, Lignosus rhinocerus, Ophiocordyceps sinensis, Phellinus linteus, Pleurotus ostreatus, Taiwanofungus camphoratus
Cardiovascular Disease	Agaricus bisporus
Cognitive Function	Agaricus bisporus, Hericium erinaceus, Flammulina velutipes
Depression	Hericium erinaceus
Diabetes	Agaricus subrufescens, Agaricus campestris, Coriolus versicolor, Fomitopsis pinicola, Grifola frondosa, Hericium erinaceus, Inonotuus obliquus, Ophiocordyceps sinensis, Phellinus linteus, Pleurotus ostreatus, Pleurotus tuber-regium, Taiwanofungus camphoratus
Digestion	Hericium erinaceus
Endurance	Ophiocordyceps sinensis
Fatigue	Agaricus campestris, Ophiocordyceps sinensis, Taiwanofungus camphoratus
Fungal Diseases	Pleurotus ostreatus
Gastrointestinal Issues	Ophiocordyceps sinensis
General Well-Being	Ophiocordyceps sinensis
Gut Health	Agaricus bisporus

Headache	Fomitopsis pincola
Hemorrhaging	Fomitopsis betulina, Panellus stipticus
Hepatitis B	Agaricus subrufescens, Taiwanofungus camphoratus
Hepatitis C	Inonotuus obliquus
High Cholesterol	Auricularia auricula-judae, Flammulina velutipes, Laetiporus sulphureus, Lentinula edodes, Pleurotus ostreatus
HIV	Fomitopsis betulina, Inonotuus obliquus
Hypertension	Flammulina velutipes, Pleurotus cornucopiae
Hypoglycemia	Auricularia auricula-judae, Inonotuus obliquus, Laetiporus sulphureus
Immune System	Coriolus versicolor, Flammulina velutipes, Lentinula edodes, Ophiocordyceps sinensis, Taiwanofungus camphoratus
Inflammation	Agaricus subrufescens, Auricularia auricula-judae, Flammulina velutipes, Fomitopsis betulina, Fomitopsis pincola, Ganoderma lucidum, Hericium erinaceus, Laetiporus sulphureus, Lignosus rhinocerus, Phellinus linteus
Insomnia	Ganoderma lucidum
Irritable Bowel Syndrome (IBS)	Grifola frondosa, Hericium erinaceus,
Kidney Function	Ophiocordyceps sinensis
Lesions	Pleurotus ostreatus
Libido	Ophiocordyceps sinensis
Liver Issues	Ganoderma lucidum, Laetiporus sulphureus, Lignosus rhinocerus
Malaria	Agaricus subrufescens, Laetiporus sulphureus

Memory	Hericium erinaceus
Menopause	Hericium erinaceus
Myocardial Ischemia-Reperfusion (IR)	Phellinus linteus
Nerve Regeneration	Hericium erinaceus, Lignosus rhinocerus
Neurodegenerative Diseases	Flammulina velutipes, Phellinus linteus
Neuropathy	Hericium erinaceus
Obesity	Lignosus rhinocerus
Parkinson's	Hericium erinaceus
Pulmonary Diseases	Fomitopsis officinalis
Purgative	Fomitopsis betulina
Respiratory Issues	Ganoderma lucidum, Pleurotus ostreatus
Skin Care	Fomitopsis betulina, Fomitopsis pinicola
Sore Throat	Auricularia auricula-judae
Stamina	Ophiocordyceps sinensis
Staph Infection	Laetiporus sulphureus
Strength	Hericium erinaceus
Tick-Borne Encephalitis (TBE)	Fomitopsis betulina
Tuberculosis	Fomitopsis officinalis
Tumors	Agaricus subrufescens, Auricularia auricula-judae, Grifola frondosa, Inonotuus obliquus, Lentinula edodes, Pleurotus ostreatus
Ulcers	Hericium erinaceus, Laetiporus sulphureus
Urinary Tract	Ganoderma lucidum

Vigor	Hericium erinaceus
Viruses	Fomitopsis betulina, Phellinus linteus, Pleurotus ostreatus, Pleurotus tuber-regium
Wounds	Hericium erinaceus

if there is a specific cancer the mushroom is recommended for as treatment, it is detailed in the cancer section below.

Many of the diseases in this chart are related; for example, often tumors and cancers are related, and aging and antioxidants have a strong correlation. They are separated here because of the studies that have been done and are referenced. If you are looking for a specific disease or ailment, please scan through the list with the understanding that information may be under a different heading than expected, or it may be under several headings.

puttography/Shutterstock.com

Studies and Uses of Medicinal Mushrooms by Ailment

The majority of studies conducted on mushrooms are to test their efficacy in treating a specific disease or condition. This section details the studies done as relating to the ailment. For some, many studies traverse different mushrooms and ways of using them. With others, there are only a few studies. To understand all the information about medicinal mushroom research in regards to disease, the whole body of work should be examined.

Aging

We all age, however, how we age can be greatly improved by the addition of mushrooms into the diet. These are not miracle cures that are going to stop aging altogether, so far that isn't possible. As we age, though, our bodies lose muscle mass, our bones lose minerals, our cell membranes change, and our internal organs lose efficacy. Mushrooms can help our bodies as they transition and make them stronger and better prepared for potential age-related ailments.

Flammulina velutipes [Enoki]

Expopolysaccharides (EPS) found in F. velutipes show strong antioxidant and anti-aging properties. Polysaccharides (FPS and SFPS) studies showed increased antioxidant activities and anti-aging response.

There are two well-known types of F. velutipes in commercial production – yellow-strain and white-strain. Yellow-strain F. velutipes is a more recently developed type. A 2019 study showed yellow-strain F. velutipes to have stronger antioxidant properties than the white-strain. However, both are useful in treating age-related issues, like wrinkles, general skin aging, wound healing, and fragile skin.[77] [78]

Dosage:
Dried, 8-9 grams per day.
Fresh, 30-50 grams per day.

Pleurotus ostreatus [Oyster Mushroom]
Extracts of P. ostreatus show potential in decreasing free-radical protein oxidation which can prevent age-associated free radical disorders, like Parkinson's, cardiovascular disease, and arthritis. They have also been shown to increase antioxidant levels.[79]

Dosage:
Dried, 3-9 grams/day.
Fresh, 2-3 grams per day.
General use, 1-2 grams of extract per day.

Allergies

Suffering from allergies can be a nightmare, especially if they are intense enough to disrupt daily life. An allergic reaction is a result of the immune system objecting to something in the environment. The number of potential allergens is vast. Common allergies are to pollen, mold, insect stings, dust mites, pet dander, smoke, and specific foods.

Our immune systems go into fight mode as soon as the allergen enters our body, however, sometimes it gets overwhelmed. Symptoms include sneezing, itching, swelling, rashes, difficulty breathing, and runny nose. Reactions to allergens range from mild to severe.

Agaricus subrufescens [Almond Mushroom]

An extract of A. subrufescens, ABME (Agaricus-based Murill extract), reduced the release of histamine and stopped allergic swelling and inflammation when orally administered to mice. A. subrufescens extracts not only reduce allergenic symptoms, there is also evidence they can prevent allergy development. The test was conducted using IgE-mediated food allergies, which include nuts, milk, eggs, and wheat.[80]

In Japan, *Andosan* is a widely available medicine made primarily from A. subrufescens (aka A. blazei), with smaller amounts of H. erinaceus and G. frondosa, to treat allergies and asthma. Andosan was given to mice to test its efficacy in treating allergenic responses. The supplement showed it could potentially prevent allergic reactions as well as reduce symptoms of established allergies.[81]

Dosage:
Eaten fresh, 4-8oz.

Ganoderma lucidum [Reishi]

G. lucidum has been tested on allergic rhinitis in hamsters and found to inhibit nasal hyperresponsiveness and blockage with good results. In other studies, the polysaccharides naturally found in G. lucidum were shown to improve immune system function to fight against allergic reactions and the natural triterpenes suppressed histamine release. This makes G. lucidum a double-threat against allergic reactions.[82]

Ganoderma tsugae

This is the North American type of Reishi which has not been studied as thoroughly as the Asian variety, G.lucidum. A recent study using a triterpenoid extract from G. tsugae showed it has similar anti-histamine effects as well as reducing inflammation due to allergies.[83]

Dosage:
500mg extract 3x/day.

Taiwanofungus camphoratus [Stout Camphor]

Powdered T. camphoratus administered to mice showed immunomodulation effects, which means it enhanced the immune system to fight off the allergen.[84]

Dosage:
1-3 grams/day.

Alzheimer's

A debilitating disease that devastates the mind, Alzheimer's is difficult for the individual suffering and for family and friends who see their loved one lose function. This disease causes brain cells to deteriorate and eventually die. The decline in mental ability is progressive, and currently there are no cures. Alzheimer's is a disease of memory and mind. It starts slowly with forgetfulness and difficulty concentrating and progresses to forgetting names, places, and how to care for oneself. Treatments, therefore, are centered on the brain, cell health, and slowing the decline.

Hericium erinaceus [Lion's Mane]

H. erinaceus contains a compound called erinaceus. Studies show that H. erinaceus mycelium that has been enriched with an active compound delayed neuron cell death in animal studies. Specifically, it was used to treat rats with Alzheimer's, Parkinson's, Ischemic Stroke, and Depression. Not only did it delay cell death, but it also showed promise in regenerating nerves and promoting recovery from neurodegenerative diseases.[85]

In a study with wild mice, an extract of H. erinaceas reduced memory impairments, including spatial memory, visual memory, and short-term memory. [86]

Dosage:
3-5 grams/day.

Antibacterial/Antibiotic

Our world is full of bacteria, some good and some bad. There are many methods for destroying bacteria, including some things as simple as hand-washing and heat treatment. An antibacterial treatment means that it slows the growth of bacteria or kills it entirely.

The discovery of antibiotics was life-altering for humans. Fewer people died from common infections and it seemed a miracle had been discovered. Unfortunately, since their discovery, antibiotics have been used indiscriminately to treat all infections; they were overprescribed to the max and still are today. This has led to an even bigger problem: antibiotic-resistant bacteria strains.

In the almost 100 years since penicillin was discovered, the majority of antibiotics no longer work. Tuberculosis strains we thought had been eliminated, or that were at least under control, are now re-emerging stronger than before.

Not all bacteria are bad. In fact, we need good bacteria in our bodies to balance out the bad.

The combination of antibiotic use and antibacterial soaps, sprays, and more have created a culture in which we kill all bacteria, whether good or bad.

Mushrooms offer a unique opportunity for fixing this problem we have created, if we are careful. Penicillin, after all, is a fungi mold that has been overused and we need to be aware and not let that happen again. The antibacterial properties of mushrooms are varied and potentially can be used to fight specific bacteria instead of killing off all bacteria.

Fomitopsis betulina [Birch Polypore]

Lab studies testing the efficacy of F. betulina against varied bacteria showed strong activity. Bacteria types submitted to testing include Staph, Candida, E.coli, and Bacillus.[87]

Studies show F. betulina contains piptamine, which is a natural antibiotic and has been used to treat E. coli. This mushroom also contains polyporenic acids and triterpenoids which fight against bacteria.[88]

Dosage:
General use 1 teaspoon tincture twice a day.
Tea, 2-3 8oz cups per day (3-12 grams dried mushroom).

Anticoagulant

Anticoagulants are blood thinners that prevent blood clots from forming. Blood clots are serious and can lead to heart attacks, strokes, and death.

There are anticoagulants available today that work well, however, they tend to have serious side-effects. For example, the drug Warfarin warns of bruising, dark or bloody stools, nasal and gum bleeding and coughing up blood. Finding an alternative that does not express such undesirable side-effects is of great interest to researchers around the world.

Auricularia auricula-judae [Jelly Ear Fungus]

In a 2019 study of anticoagulant activities of mushrooms, it was discovered that A. auricula-judae contains an acid polysaccharide with anticoagulant properties.[89]

Dosage:
Eaten fresh, 1-2 oz.
General-use, 2-3 grams of extract per day.

Ganoderma lucidum [Reishi]

A study done in 2019 demonstrated that G. lucidum makes a metalloprotease that contains the potential for preventing blood clots.[90]

Dosage:
Tea, 100-200ml/day (3/4 cup).
Tincture, 2-3 droppers per day (2-3ml total) or for targeted use, 10ml 3x/day.
Dried or Fresh, 3-5 grams/day.

Hydnellum peckii [Devil's Tooth]

A 2019 study of several mushroom species to evaluate their use as an anticoagulant demonstrated that H. peckii contains a natural anticoagulant called atromentin. It is similar to the widely known and widely used anticoagulant, heparin.[91]

Dosage:
Not available commercially.

Laetiporus sulphureus [Chicken of the Woods]

An extract from L. sulphureus exhibited anticoagulant properties and needs to be studied further to determine efficacy.[92]

Dosage:
Fresh, 4-6 oz. per day.

Lignosus rhinocerus [Tiger's Milk]

Extracts of L. rhinocerotis demonstrated anticoagulant abilities as well as fibrinolytic activity (a process that prevents blood clots).[93]

Dosage:
General use, 250-500 mg/day.

Antimicrobial (Infections, Bacteria, Virus, Fungal)

Like antibiotics, antimicrobial medicines have been overused and over-prescribed. Many bacteria, viruses, and disease-causing organisms have developed resistance and are stronger now than they were 100 years ago when penicillin was first discovered. The more the drugs are overused, the quicker the infectious organisms develop resistance. Currently, the situation is quite dire and the race to find new antimicrobial treatments that can fight the drug-resistant strains is in full swing.

Mushrooms offer a unique opportunity to develop a variety of natural antimicrobial agents. Like all things, however, our use has to be monitored so the same scenario is not recreated. Penicillin is the fungi-mold that started the antibiotic age and our over-reliance on it should be used as a warning. Having a wide range of options is better, which makes research into all the fungi types extremely important.

Research shows different levels of efficacy with various mushrooms in treating specific types of infections (bacterial or viral or fungal) and some mushrooms that show viability in being used for more generalized applications. (See also Viruses.)

Agaricus bisporus [Button Mushroom]
Research demonstrates the significant antimicrobial properties of A. bisporus, specifically in treating Staph infections.[94]

Dosage:
Eaten fresh, 4-8oz.

Agaricus campestris [Field Mushroom]

A study in 2017 showed that A. campestris has strong antimicrobial activity.[95]

Dosage:

Eaten fresh, 4-8oz.

Agaricus subrufescens [Almond Mushroom]

An extract of A. subrufescens given to mice demonstrated use in treating pneumonia. It shows promise in use as a prophylactic (preventing disease) and potential in therapeutically treating bacterial and other infections.[96]

Dosage:

Eaten fresh, 4-8oz.

Flammulina velutipes [Enoki]

Multiple studies have shown F. velutipes extracts and components demonstrate strong antimicrobial properties:[97]

- Staph
- Bacillus subtilis
- Bacillus pumilus
- Pseudomonas aeruginosa, a pathogen resistant to many drugs that proliferates chronic infections of the skin, after surgery or severe burns, as well as treating urinary tract and respiratory infections
- Sporothrix schenckii
- Candida albicans

Dosage:
Dried, 8-9 grams per day.
Fresh, 30-50 grams per day.

Fomitopsis betulina [Birch Polypore]
Extracts, or direct application, of F. betulina to wounds or cuts, have shown antiseptic effectiveness.[98]

Dosage:
General use 1 teaspoon tincture twice a day.
Tea, 2-3 8oz cups per day (3-12 grams dried mushroom).

Fomitopsis officinalis [Agarikon]
The antimicrobial properties have been established in several studies. Research suggests it is due to triterpenoids present in the fungi. Compared to other fungi, F. officinalis has higher antimicrobial properties and potential for treating viral and bacterial infections.[99]

Agaricin (agaric acid), a compound in F. officinalis, is anti-inflammatory, parasympatholytic (relating to the nervous system, and anhidrotic (relating to sweating). It is produced synthetically by several pharmaceutical companies.[100]

A study of bees and colony collapse syndrome demonstrated F. officinalis has antibacterial and antiviral properties which could prove useful in many situations.[101]

Dosage:

General use, 10-20 grams per day.

Fomitopsis pincola [Red-banded Polypore]
Extracts of F. pincola have shown efficacy in lab studies for fighting Bacillus infections.[102]

Dosage:
General use, 20-30 grams twice daily.

Inonotuus obliquus [Chaga]
Extracts of I. obliquus have demonstrated efficacy in combating Francisella tularensis, a pathogen that can cause a lethal form of pneumonia. It has also shown the ability to treat oral bacterial infections.[103]

Dosage:
Dried, 1/2 teaspoon per day (2.5oz).
Tincture, 2-3 droppers per day (2-3ml total).
Tea, 1-2 6oz cups per day.

Laetiporus sulphureus [Chicken of the Woods]
Water-ethanol extractions of L. sulphureus demonstrated the ability to fight bacterial and fungal infections:[104]

- Staph
- Bacillus bacteria, common in intestinal illness
- Enterobacter cloacae, a germ that is often contracted during hospitalization, causing urinary tract, eye, and endocardium (heart) infections. It is also responsible for blood poisoning and skin, organ, respiratory, and tissue inflammation

- E. Coli, which affects the intestinal tract
- Listeria
- Pseudomonas aeruginosa, a common bacteria that proliferate chronic infections of the skin, after surgery or severe burns, as well as urinary tract and respiratory infections
- Salmonella
- Proteus vulgaris, which can cause urinary tract infections
- Candida, a fungal infection

Dosage:
Fresh, 4-6 oz. per day.

Lentinula edodes [Shiitake]
Extracts of L. edodes were lab-tested against 29 bacterial and 10 fungal pathogens. The extract demonstrates significant antimicrobial activity against 85% of the pathogens.[105]

Dosage:
Fresh, 3-5 oz. /day.
Dried, 2-6 grams/day.

Phellinus linteus [Black Hoof Mushroom]
Extracts of P. linteus demonstrated efficacy in treating several strains of Staph infection as well as MRSA. Additionally, it showed great potential in treating porphyromonas gingivalis, which is the leading cause of chronic periodontal disease and which was recently discovered to be a potential proponent in rheumatoid arthritis and Alzheimer's disease. P. linteus also may be

an effective treatment against influenza.[106]

Dosage:
Dried, 10-30 grams per day.
General use, 2-3 grams extract per day.

Pleurotus ostreatus [Oyster Mushroom]
Methanol extracts of P. ostreatus were successful in inhibiting the growth of bacterial and fungal diseases:[107]
- E. coli
- Bacillus megaterium
- Staph
- Klebsiella pneumoniae bacteria (found in the gut, can cause severe infection when spread outside the gut)
- Candida albicans
- Candida glabrata
- Trichophyton
- Epidermophyton

Dosage:
Dried, 3-9 grams/day.
Fresh, 2-3 grams per day.

Tricholoma matsutake [Matsutake]
Several studies have demonstrated the antimicrobial properties of T. matsutake.[108]

Dosage:
Fresh or dried, 4-8 oz. /per day.

Antioxidant

An antioxidant is a natural or man-made substance that delays or prevents cell damage. They are found naturally in many foods, including mushrooms. Consuming larger amounts of antioxidants has been shown to potentially protect the body from some diseases. Additionally, it is thought the free-radical fighting properties of antioxidants improve skin, overall health, and prevents age-related decline.

All mushrooms contain some concentration of antioxidants, some more than others.

Agaricus subrufescens [Almond Mushroom]
Extracts of A. subrufescens were tested in the lab for their antioxidant properties and were found to contain high amounts.[109]

Dosage:
Eaten fresh, 4-8oz.

Agaricus bisporus [Button Mushroom]
In a study comparing antioxidant properties of mushrooms, A. bisporus showed higher levels than L. edodes, P. ostreatus, and G. frondosa.[110]

Dosage:
Eaten fresh, 4-8oz.

Agaricus campestris [Field Mushroom]
The antioxidant properties were evaluated in a 2017 study and free radical and superoxide scavenging abilities were strong.[111]

Dosage:
Eaten fresh, 4-8oz.

Auricularia auricula-judae [Jelly Ear Fungus]

In lab studies, A. auricula-judae demonstrated antioxidant properties that were dose-dependent.[112]

Dosage:
Eaten fresh, 1-2 oz.
General-use, 2-3 grams extract per day.

Flammulina velutipes [Enoki]

Expopolysaccharides (EPS) and Polysaccharides (FPS and SFPS) studies of F. velutipes show strong antioxidant and anti-aging properties.[113] [114]

Dosage:
Dried, 8-9 grams per day.
Fresh, 30-50 grams per day.

Ganoderma lucidum [Reishi]

Antioxidant properties were significant in lab-studies conducted in 2015.[115]

Dosage:
Tea, 100-200ml/day (3/4 cup).
Tincture, 2-3 droppers per day (2-3ml total) or for targeted use, 10ml 3x/day.
Dried or Fresh, 3-5 grams/day.

Inonotuus obliquus [Chaga]

Research conducted with mice showed the

polysaccharides in I. obliquus have antioxidant properties.[116]

Dosage:
Dried, 1/2 teaspoon per day (2.5oz).
Tincture, 2-3 droppers per day (2-3ml total).
Tea, 1-2 6oz cups per day.

Laetiporus sulphureus [Chicken of the Woods]
An extract of L. sulphureus demonstrated high antioxidant activity, even preventing hepatitis from occurring in test animals. The strong antioxidant properties are assigned to the presence of oxalic acid. Of mushrooms currently tested, L. sulphureus has the second-highest levels of antioxidant properties, with G. lucidum coming in first.[117]

Dosage:
Fresh, 4-6 oz. per day.

Ophiocordyceps sinensis [Cordyceps]
Extracts studied in lab settings demonstrate that O. sinensis has high antioxidant properties. Wild foraged and cultivated O. sinensis showed equal antioxidant potential.[118]

Dosage:
Tea, 100ml (1/3 cup) per day.
General use, 2-3 grams per day.

Phellinus linteus [Black Hoof Mushroom]
Lab and animal-based research have demonstrated the

antioxidant properties of P. linteus. The polysaccharides and hispidin components of the fungi are thought to be the triggering factors.[119]

Dosage:
Dried, 10-30 grams per day.
General use, 2-3 grams extract per day.

Pleurotus ostreatus [Oyster Mushroom]
In studies on the properties of P. ostreatus, the mushroom has demonstrated strong antioxidant abilities due to the polysaccharide pleuran.[120]

Dosage:
Dried, 3-9 grams/day.
Fresh, 2-3 grams per day.

Taiwanofungus camphoratus [Stout Camphor Fungus]
An extract of T. camphoratus was studied for its antioxidant properties and was shown to possess them.[121]

Dosage:
1-3 grams/day.

Anxiety

A small amount of anxiety or fear is normal in everyday life. Anxiety disorders, like OCD, Panic disorder, PTSD, and general anxiety disorder can disrupt life in many ways. There are numerous medications available as prescribed by a doctor to relieve these symptoms. They all have side-effects, though, that can be just as debilitating. The use of mushrooms, in combination with therapy, may be a better option.

Hericium erinaceus [Lion's Mane]

A two-month study with mice showed improved recognition memory. Recognition memory is the ability to determine what is familiar and what is new, or novel. Subjects with weak recognition memory are at risk of anxiety and depression. Their inability to cope with unfamiliar objects correlates to their mental well-being. In this study, the mice sought out new experiences while administered H. erinaceus, which indicates reduced anxiety.[122]

Dosage:

Tea, 100ml 2-3 times per day (1/3 cup).
Dried, 3-5 grams per day.

Arthritis (incl. Rheumatoid)

Pain, stiffness, and swelling of the joints are signs of arthritis. Arthritis affects a large proportion of the population and can severely limit a person's ability to do things. Swollen joints, over time, can become damaged and some arthritis causes issues with other organs, like eyes and skin.

There are several types of arthritis; Osteoarthritis is usually age-related or occurs due to injury. Autoimmune arthritis, like Rheumatism, is caused by the immune system overreacting. Psoriasis arthritis is a type that occurs along with psoriasis.

Fomitopsis officinalis [Agarikon]

The antimicrobial and anti-inflammatory actions of F. officinalis are speculated to provide efficacy in treating rheumatoid arthritis.[123]

Dosage:

General use, 10-20 grams per day.

Ganoderma lucidum [Reishi]

Researchers have tested the efficacy of an anti-inflammatory supplement made up of G. lucidum and San-Miao-San. Patients with rheumatoid arthritis took the capsules, and results demonstrated the capsules may improve immune function.[124] It is unclear whether the G. lucidum or San-Miao-San was the catalyst for improvement or whether they both contributed.

Dosage:

For rheumatoid arthritis, 1-3 grams extract per day.

Asthma

A chronic disease that causes the lungs to become sore and swollen, asthma affects a significant portion of the population. Treatments for asthma are either quick-acting, to stop an attack, or long-acting, to prevent them from happening. Several mushrooms show good potential in reducing or eliminating asthma symptoms and occurrences.

Ganoderma lucidum [Reishi]

Due to its ability to fight allergies and strengthen the immune system, many naturalists suggest G. lucidum for treating asthma as well. (See sections on Allergies and Inflammation). Currently, no medical studies are validating this specific use.

Dosage:
For asthma, 1-3 grams extract per day.

Fomitopsis officinalis [Agarikon]

The anti-inflammatory and antimicrobial actions of F. officinalis are suggested as having potential in treating asthma. Traditional Chinese medicine has been prescribing these fungi for asthma and allergies for centuries.[125]

Dosage:
General use, 10-20 grams per day.

Lignosus rhinocerus [Tiger's Milk]

An extract of L. rhinocerus was administered intranasally in mice with induced allergic asthma. The study demonstrated that the extract reduced airway inflammation when applied nasally.[126]

Dosage:
General use, 250-500 mg/day.

Pleurotus ostreatus [Oyster Mushroom]

In a study of children with Recurrent Respiratory Tract Infections (RRTI), those administered an extract of P. ostreatus showed reduced allergic reactions.[127]

Dosage:

General use, 1-2 grams extract per day.

Cancer

A multi-faceted disease that can cause multiple symptoms and problems, cancer is the number one killer currently. There have been hundreds of studies into the effectiveness of different mushrooms in treating cancer occurrences and symptoms, including their usefulness as an adjunct used in combination with chemotherapy. Some mushrooms have shown better potency with specific types of cancer while others have demonstrated a more generalized use.

CANCER TYPE	MUSHROOM (listed alphabetically, not based on effectiveness)
Breast	Agaricus bisporus, Flammulina velutipes, Fomitopsis betulina, Grifola frondosa, Lignosus rhinocerus, Pleurotus ostreatus
Cervical	Flammulina velutipes, Inonotus obliquus, Lignosus rhinocerus
Colon	Agaricus campestris, Coriolus versicolor, Fomitopsis betulina, Grifola frondosa, Inonotus obliquus, Lentinula edodes, Phellinus linteus, Pleurotus ostreatus
Head & Neck (nasopharyngeal)	Flammunlia velutipes
Leukemia	Agaricus bisporus, Ganoderma lucidum, Inonotus obliquus, Phellinus linteus
Liver	Agaricus subrufescens, Flammulina velutipes, Grifola frondosa, Inonotus obliquus, Lentinula edodes, Ophiocordyceps sinensis, Phellinus linteus, Taiwanofungus camphoratus

Lung	Agaricus campestris, Fomitopsis betulina, Grifola frondosa, Lignosus rhinocerus, Lentinula edodes, Ophiocordyceps sinensis
Metastatic	Ganoderma lucidum
Ovarian	Ganoderma lucidum
Pancreatic	Phellinus linteus
Prostrate	Lignosus rhinocerus, Phellinus linteus
Sarcoma	Phellinus linteus
Skin	Ophiocordyceps sinensis
Stomach (Gastric)	Coriolus, versicolor, Flammulina velutipes, Lentinula edodes
Non-Specific	Coriolus versicolor, Fomitopsis pinicola, Ganoderma lucidum, Laetiporus sulphureus, Lentinula edodes, Ophiocordyceps sinensis, Phellinus linteus, Taiwanofungus camphoratus

Agaricus subrufescens [Almond Mushroom]

The polysaccharides in A. subrufescens have shown to hold antitumor properties.

Currently, between 300k-500k people in Japan take 3-5g of extracted A. subrufescens 3x/day along with chemotherapy to prevent or treat cancer.[128]

Extracts of A. subrufescens have demonstrated efficacy in treating liver cancer. Gynecological cancer patients who took a daily dose of A. subrufescens while concurrently going through chemotherapy showed improved cancer-killing cell activities and increased quality of life.

A daily extract of this mushroom given to cancer patients in remission showed an improved quality of life. Increased life expectancy was not shown.

There have been a few deaths of patients with severe liver damage after taking A. subrufescens, although it can't be said with certainty that the extract directly caused the deaths.[129]

Dosage:
For cancer, 3 grams per day.

Agaricus bisporus [Button Mushroom]
A 2010 study compared A. bisporus against Pleurotus ostreatus and Grifola frondosa in an experiment treating breast cancer. While P. ostreatus and G. frondosa performed better than A. bisporus, they were all effective at reducing the expansion of breast cancer cells. Three variations of A. bisporus were tested – crimini, portobello, and white button. [130]

A bisporus demonstrates capabilities to stimulate the immune system as well as fight cancers. It produces lovastatin, which is used to treat high cholesterol and has shown promise in fighting breast cancer. Additionally, it offers hope in fighting leukemia.[131]

The Canadian Cancer Society is investing in research involving A. bisporus in treating and/or preventing breast cancer.[132]

Dosage:

Eaten fresh, 4-8oz.

Agaricus campestris [Field Mushroom]

A lab study in 2017 on the effects of an extract of A. campestris on lung and colon carcinoma cells showed the extract to have cell-killer abilities.[133]

Dosage:

Eaten fresh, 4-8oz.

Coriolus versicolor [Turkey Tail]

Extracts of C. versicolor have shown many anti-cancer activities. In a study of patients who underwent surgery for stomach and colon cancer, PSK (the polysaccharide extract) benefited the patients by improving survival rates. In breast, liver, and leukemia cancers, there was no noticeable effect.

PSK, in animal trials, reduced the immune-suppression effects of chemotherapy and radiation.[134] [135]

Dosage:

For cancer, 3-6 grams extract per day.
For immune support, 1-2 grams extract per day.

Flammulina velutipes [Enoki]

A lab study in 2006 tested 38 species of mushrooms to see if any had viability in treating breast cancer. F. velutipes was one of three that showed promise in fighting tumor cells.[136]

In 2006, an extract of F. velutipes, labeled flammulinol,

was found to have cell-death effects against several cancers, including cervical, liver, and nasopharyngeal (head and neck).[137]

Additionally, lab studies in 2012 and 2013 showed the efficacy of F. velutipe extracts in killing liver, breast, lung, and gastric cancers.[138]

Dosage:
Dried, 8-9 grams per day.
Fresh, 30-50 grams per day.

Ganoderma lucidum [Reishi]
In 2001, a study was conducted to evaluate G. lucidum extract uses in treating ovarian cancer. Results demonstrated G. lucidum was effective in inhibiting the growth of cancer cells. In addition, when combined with cisplatin (a chemotherapy drug), the results were considerably enhanced.[139]

G. lucidum extracts were tested for their efficacy in elevating the immune-system in advanced cancer patients with different cancers. This 2003 12-week study showed that G. lucidum enhanced immune responses in these patients.[140]

Extracts of G. lucidum were tested for their efficacy in relieving nausea and vomiting during chemotherapy treatments (specifically against cisplatin, a chemotherapy drug). The 2005 study on rats determined G. lucidum was supportive and should be studied further for its specific usefulness.[141]

Researchers in 2008 discovered G. lucidum increased the effectiveness of radiation treatments in treating leukemia. They suggest it could be used therapeutically in conjunction with radiotherapy.[142]

Results of a 2008 study showed a component of G. lucidum, ganoderic acid, inhibited tumor growth and shows potential in treating metastatic cancer.[143]

A lab study done on the potentially toxic effects of G. lucidum treatments on children's cancer in 2008 determined there was some toxicity and therefore, cautious use is recommended.[144]

A 2012 study on how G. lucidum affects the survival rates of cancer patients found no evidence that it affected longevity. However, cancer patients taking it showed improved quality of life.[145]

Dosage:
For cancer, 2-5 grams extract per day.

Grifola frondosa [Hen of the Woods]
A study of cancer patients in 2002 investigated the effectiveness of treating symptoms with G. frondosa. Stage II-IV cancer patients were given a range of doses and symptoms and cancer regression were monitored.
- Liver cancer – 58% of patients showed a significant reduction of symptoms or regression
- Breast cancer – 68.8% of patients showed a significant reduction of symptoms or regression

- Lung cancer – 62.5% of patients showed a significant reduction of symptoms or regression
- Leukemia, stomach cancer, and brain cancer patients showed less than 10-20% improvement

Additionally, patients taking G. frondosa alongside chemotherapy demonstrated enhanced anticancer activity as compared to chemotherapy alone.[146]

Research conducted in 2010 demonstrated extracts of G. frondosa showed potential in treating tumors associated with colon cancer.[147]

A study in 2010 comparing G. frondosa to Pleurotus ostreatus and Agaricus bisporus showed G. frondosa and P. ostreatus to be the most effective in killing breast cancer cells. G. frondosa was the most effective at apoptosis, programmed cell death. All mushrooms tested reduced cellular proliferation of breast cancer cells.[148]

Lab studies conducted in 2017 determined polysaccharides in G. frondosa killed human breast cancer cells and show enormous potential as a treatment for breast cancer.[149]

Dosage:
Fresh, 3-7 grams/day or more.
For PCOS (polycystic ovary syndrome), 3 grams per day.

Fomitopsis betulina [Birch Polypore]

Extracts of F. betulina were used in lab tests for their efficacy against colon, lung, and breast cancers. They showed the ability to inhibit cell growth and prevent more from growing in all three cases. [150]

Before modern medical practices, and continuing today, a tea of F. betulina was used to treat cancer in Siberia, Finland, and the Baltics.[151]

Dosage:
General use, 1 teaspoon tincture twice a day.
Tea, 2-3 8oz cups per day (3-12 grams dried mushroom).

Fomitopsis pinicola [Red-banded Polypore]
Studies show the polysaccharides in F. pincola have mild anti-tumor properties as well as abilities to stimulate the immune system. [152]

In Japan, it is used widely as a cancer preventative and fighter. In lab studies comparing F. pincola with Ganoderma lucidum (Reishi) and F. officinalis (Agarikon), F. pincola demonstrated more efficacy than both the others.[153]

Dosage:
General use, 20-30 grams twice daily.

Inonotus obliquus [Chaga]
Studies have demonstrated the potential of I. obliquus extracts in treating cervical, colon, leukemia, and liver tumors.[154]

Dosage:
For cancer, 2-5 grams extract per day.

Laetiporus sulphureus [Chicken of the Woods]
A compound found in L. sulphureus, laetirobin (named for the mushroom) stopped cancer cells from reproducing and terminated the ones already there. Additionally, the polysaccharides in L. sulphureus have demonstrated abilities to fight cancer.[155]

Dosage:
Fresh, 4-6 oz. per day.

Lentinula edodes [Shiitake]
Lentinan, a sugar molecule found in L. edodes, has demonstrated effectiveness at extending the survival of liver, stomach, pancreatic, and colon cancer patients. Additionally, it was shown to be effective in prolonging survival in the liver and gastric cancer patients who used it in combination with chemotherapy treatments. Lung cancer patients showed improved quality of life.

Lentinan based supplements are available in some countries for clinical use as therapeutic agents for cancer treatments.

An extract from Basidiomycete-type mushrooms, which includes L. edodes, possesses a compound called AHCC. Preliminary studies of this compound show immunomodulatory actions as well as antioxidant and anti-inflammatory properties and it is being studied as a cancer treatment.[156]

AHCC was administered to human liver cancer patients following surgical treatments in a 2002 study. Those taking AHCC went longer between recurrences and had an increased survival rate.[157]

Dosage:
For immune support, 2-6 grams extract per day.

Lignosus rhinocerus [Tiger's Milk]

Studies conducted on various concentrations and extracts of L. rhinocerus proved to affect several cancers, including cervical cancer, lung carcinoma, prostate, and breast cancer. The cold water extraction method proved efficacy at reducing solid tumors while the hot water extraction did not do anything.[158]

Dosage:
General use, 250-500 mg/day.

Ophiocordyceps sinensis [Cordyceps]

In a 1999 study, an extract of O. sinensis was used to treat liver metastasis in mice with Lewis lung carcinoma. The extract displayed strong antitumor activity.[159]

Researchers in 2007 studied the effects of cordycepin, an extract of O. sinensis, on skin cancer cells. The results showed the extract induced cell death of skin cancer cells.[160]

An extract of O. sinensis was tested for its efficacy in

reducing the damage caused by radiotherapy in cancer treatments. Specifically, bone marrow and intestinal damage were studied. In the study, mice receiving the treatment were protected from damage to bone marrow and intestinal damage and life expectancy increased. The results were dependent on the dose of radiotherapy the mice received.[161]

A 2011 study examined the effects of an O. sinensis polysaccharide in treating non-small cell lung cancer as well as investigating how it works in conjunction with cisplatin, a chemotherapy treatment. Results showed that cells treated with O. sinensis in addition to cisplatin inhibited tumor growth and showed significantly better results than cisplatin treatment on its own.[162]

Dosage:
For cancer, 2-5 grams extract per day.

Phellinus linteus [Black Hoof Mushroom]
The polysaccharides in P. linteus have shown anticancer activity in both lab and animal studies. Specifically, they showed promise in treating colon and sarcoma cancers and reducing tumors.

Additional studies demonstrated that the hispolon properties have efficacy in treating leukemia as well as broadly fighting other cancers.[163] [164]

In a study of pancreatic cancer patients, P. linteus demonstrated potential as an adjunct therapy in combination with chemotherapy. In studies of liver and prostate cancer, P. linteus demonstrated regressive properties.[165]

Dosage:
Dried, 10-30 grams per day.
General use, 2-3 grams extract per day.

Pleurotus ostreatus [Oyster Mushroom]
A 2006 study of P. ostreatus DNA and its effects in treating mice with Ehrlich carcinoma demonstrated an increase in cytotoxic activity (killing cells) and the life span of the mice was significantly increased.[166] Ehrlich carcinoma tumors occur exclusively in the mammary glands of mice.

A 2008 study compared the ability of P. ostreatus in combating colon and breast cancers in comparison to Agaricus bisporus, Flammulina velutipes, and Lentinula edodes. P. ostreatus was effective at inhibiting the growth of colon and breast cancer cells and performed significantly better than the other mushrooms.[167]

A 2010 study comparing the efficacy of several mushroom extracts on breast cancer cells showed P. ostreatus, along with Grifola frondosa, were the best at reducing the proliferation of breast cancer cells. The other mushroom tested, Agaricus bisporus (in Crimini, Portobello, and White Button forms) was effective as well.[168]

Another study in 2010 researched the effectiveness of treating colon cancer in mice with P. ostreatus. Results

110

were dose-dependent, with a higher dose of 500mg reducing the occurrence of colon tumors by 50%. Abnormal cells and colon shortening were also significantly reduced.[169]

Dosage:
Dried, 3-9 grams/day.
Fresh, 2-3 grams per day.

Taiwanofungus camphoratus [Stout Camphor Fungus]
An extract of T. camphoratus was lab-tested in treating liver cancer cells as well as used in combination with common chemotherapy drugs. On its own, T. camphoratus demonstrated tumor-fighting abilities. When used in combination with cisplatin and doxorubicin, it demonstrated enhanced tumor suppression.[170]

A 2012 study in Taiwan identified eleven elements of interest in T. camphoratus. The most noteworthy was a triterpenoid labeled MAA (methyl antcinate A). MAA demonstrated potent cell-death properties on liver, oral, and prostate cancer cells.[171]

Dosage:
For liver disease and cancer, 1-3 grams extract per day.

Cardiovascular

When fat and cholesterol build up in blood vessels, the vessels begin to narrow, causing extreme problems with the heart.

Heart attack and stroke are common occurrences with bad cardiovascular health. Several mushrooms show potential in reducing overall cholesterol (see High Cholesterol section for more on that specifically) and reducing build-up in the blood vessels.

Agaricus bisporus [Button Mushroom]
The anti-diabetic properties combined with the effects of cholesterol are significant in improving heart health.

Dosage:
Eaten fresh, 4-8oz.

Ganoderma lucidum [Reishi]
A 2016 study of G. lucidum extracts found that they reduced the potential of heart failure in mice by reducing fatty plaque deposits in the arteries.[172]

Dosage:
For cardiovascular health, 1-3 grams extract per day.

Ophiocordyceps sinensis [Cordyceps]
Patients with chronic heart failure showed improvement after taking O. sinensis, as demonstrated by EKG (ECG) tests. Blood circulation to the essential organs was improved.[173]

Dosage:
Tea, 100ml (1/3 cup) per day.
General use, 2-3 grams per day.

Cognitive Function

As we age, our cognitive abilities naturally decline. A good diet and plenty of exercise seem to be important factors in maintaining good cognitive function over the years. For some, though, genetic predisposition or other diseases can reduce cognitive function even when good health is maintained. Reduced cognitive function can be the first sign of dementia or Alzheimer's. Several mushrooms show promise in improving overall cognitive function and potentially preventing or slowing down the advancement of progressive diseases.

Improving cognitive function isn't just for elderly people, though. Everyone can benefit from a boost to the brain and memory. Anyone who struggles with memory or motor skills can be helped.

Agaricus bisporus [Button Mushroom]
An 8-week study on rats in 2015 showed adding A. bisporus to the diet improved working memory, balance, motor function, and cognitive ability.[174]

Dosage:
Eaten fresh, 4-8oz.

Hericium erinaceus [Lion's Mane]
A study of 50-80-year-old Japanese women and men with mild cognitive impairment were given 250mg tablets of powdered H. erinaceus three times a day for 16 weeks. Their cognitive function improved significantly during that time. Four weeks after stopping the treatment, however, their cognitive function had decreased again. [175]

Dosage:
For Alzheimer's, 3-5 grams/day.

Flammulina velutipes [Enoki]
A 2011 lab study demonstrated extracts of F. velutipes had potential in enhancing learning and cognitive ability.[176]

Dosage:
For neurodegenerative issues, 3-5 grams per day.

Depression

A serious disease that affects almost everyone in varying forms of intensity, depression symptoms should not be taken lightly. For some, a small boost is sufficient for coming out of a depression, but for others, it takes much stronger medicine, therapy, and other treatments. Most prescription medicines for depression have serious side effects on internal organs and can cause serious health issues after long periods of intake.

The search for a more natural cure without serious side-effects is extremely important as more and more people take medication or self-medicate with harmful substances. There aren't a lot of studies of mushrooms and their effects on depression but the ones done with H. erinaceus show enormous potential.

Hericium erinaceus [Lion's Mane]
H. erinaceus mycelium enriched with erinacines (a natural element of the fungi) was used to treat chronic repeated stress in mice. In the two-week study, the

stress-related symptoms were reversed. Dopamine, serotonin, and epinephrine levels were affected and regulated.[177]

A 4-week clinical study of menopausal women showed reduced anxiety and depression, specifically reduced irritation, improved concentration, and less anxiety. [178]
Also see section on Memory, for a discussion on recognition memory as it relates to depression.

Dosage:
For depression, 3-5 grams/day.

Diabetes

A chronic disease in which blood glucose (blood sugar) is too high and causes serious problems affecting the heart, eyes, kidneys, and nerves. In Type 1 diabetes, the body doesn't produce insulin, which is needed to maintain proper blood glucose levels. In Type 2 diabetes (the more common type), the body does make enough insulin or doesn't use it well.

A lot of mushrooms have been studied for their potential use in treating diabetes-related health problems and for maintaining proper glucose levels.

Agaricus subrufescens [Almond Mushroom]
Several studies on mice have demonstrated potential anti-diabetic functions of A. subrufescens.[179]

Dosage:
Eaten fresh, 4-8oz.

Coriolus versicolor [Turkey Tail]

In a 2018 study, extracts of C. versicolor showed it reduced insulin resistance.[180]

A study in 2019 exhibited the effectiveness of C. versicolor in treating diabetic cardiomyopathy. Cardiac inflammation was reduced and the C. versicolor extract showed potential as a therapeutic agent.[181]

Dosage:
General use, 2-3 grams extract per day.

Fomitopsis pinicola [Birch Polypore]

Extracts of F.pinicola were tested for their efficacy in treating diabetes. They demonstrated increased insulin production and in turn, better regulation of blood sugars. They also discovered liver and kidney damage caused by diabetes may be prevented with the extract.[182]

Dosage:
General use, 20-30 grams twice daily.

Grifola frondosa [Hen of the Woods]

A study with rats demonstrated G. frondosa extracts can reduce diabetic symptoms.[183]

Dosage:
Fresh, 3-7 grams/day or more.

Hericium erinaceus [Lion's Mane]

An extract of H. erinaceus was given to diabetic rats for 28 days to investigate hypoglycemic and hypolipidemic abilities. Results showed significant effects in treating hypoglycemia and hypolipidemia.[184]

A study of rats and the effects of H. erinaceus against diabetic neuropathy demonstrated increased pain relief and alleviation of symptoms. Additionally, serum glucose and urine sugar levels were lowered. The overall diabetic state was also improved. [185]

Dosage:
Tea, 100ml 2-3 times per day (1/3 cup).
Dried, 3-5 grams per day.

Inonotus obliquus [Chaga]
Studies on diabetic mice demonstrated the ability of polysaccharides in I. obliquus to lower blood cholesterol levels as well as reduce triglycerides, glucose, and fatty acids. Additional studies showed it possesses hypoglycemic action.[186]

Dosage:
Dried, 1/2 teaspoon per day (2.5oz).
Tincture, 2-3 droppers per day (2-3ml total).
Tea, 1-2 6oz cups per day.

Laetiporus sulphureus [Chicken of the Woods]
An extract of L. sulphureus was studied on rats for its potential use in treating diabetes. It was found to increase insulinoma, which is a benign-type tumor that constantly secretes insulin. Additionally, another

compound in the L. sulphureus fruiting body, called dehydrametetenolic acid was found to reduce hyperglycemia levels in mice with non-insulin dependent diabetes. [187]

Dosage:
Fresh, 4-6 oz. per day.

Ophiocordyceps sinensis [Cordyceps]

A fermented mycelia-based broth of O. sinensis was tested for its efficacy in treating rats with diabetes. The rats displayed higher blood glucose levels and the potential for O. sinensis to be used in treating diabetes is put forward. Previous reserach studied the effects of the fruiting body of O. sinensis alone in treating hypoglycemia and diabetes-related issues with good results.[188]

A study in 2009 demonstrated that an extract of O. sinensis has the potential to suppress the onset of, or prevent, diabetes.[189]

In a 2015 study, diabetes patients with impaired renal function were given an extract of O. sinensis as a treatment for contrast-induced nephropathy (kidney damage caused by medical imaging contrast) and it was shown to be effective.[190]

Data suggests O. sinensis might work similarly to the common diabetic drug treatment metformin.[191]

Dosage:

For diabetes, 3-5 grams per day.

Phellinus linteus [Black Hoof Mushroom]

The polysaccharides and hispidin in P. linteus demonstrated an ability in inhibiting autoimmune diabetes. It showed hypoglycemic effects and could be effective in treating Type 2 diabetes.[192]

Dosage:

Dried, 10-30 grams per day.
General use, 2-3 grams extract per day.

Pleurotus cystidiosus [Abalone Oyster Mushroom]

A 2015 study investigated the effects of P. cystidiosus and P. ostreatus on patients with Type 2 diabetes and healthy human volunteers. Dried and powdered compositions of both types were administered orally. Both Pleurotus types reduced serum glucose levels and increased serum insulin levels in Type 2 diabetes patients. In healthy adults, serum glucose levels were significantly reduced postprandially (after eating a meal). In a study involving rats, both Pleurotus types allowed better absorption of glucose in the intestines and lowered serum glucose levels.[193]

Dosage:

Dried, 3-9 grams/day.
Fresh, 2-3 grams per day.

Pleurotus ostreatus [Oyster Mushroom]

In a 1993 study, insulin-dependent diabetic rats were fed a diet of 4% P. ostreatus for two months. Cholesterol was decreased by more than 40%. It did not affect levels of serum or triacylglycerols.[194]

(Also see P. cystidiosus above for a more recent study which included both Pleurotus types.)

Dosage:
Dried, 3-9 grams/day.
Fresh, 2-3 grams per day.

Pleurotus tuber-regium [Tuber Oyster Mushroom]

In 2012, a study was conducted on the effectiveness of P. tuber-regium polysaccharides in treating diabetic rats. Blood glucose levels, plasma total cholesterol, and triglycerides were significantly lowered and serum insulin levels were restored.[195]

Dosage:
Dried, 3-9 grams/day.
Fresh, 2-3 grams per day.

Taiwanofungus camphoratus [Stout Camphor Mushroom]

Extracts of T. camphoratus were tested in a lab for their usefulness in treating diabetes. Findings demonstrated increased glucose-induced insulin secretion as well as the ability to prevent Endoplasmic Reticulum (ER) stress-induced cell death. The ER is the part of a cell that functions as the manufacturing and packaging system, including that for proteins and steroids. T. camphoratus shows promise in treating Type-2 diabetes.[196]

Dosage:

1-3 grams/day.

Endurance

Increased endurance is valuable for athletes as well as non-athletes as it can assist in completing everyday tasks and help during stressful times or when energy levels are low.

Ophiocordyceps sinensis [Cordyceps]

Healthy elderly subjects, aged 50-75, were given O. sinensis capsules 3x/day for 12 weeks to test the effects it had on exercise performance. Subjects taking the capsules demonstrated a 10.5% increase in the metabolic threshold. This study was conducted in 2010.[197]

A 2015 study of O. sinensis supplementation as a way to increase endurance exercise performance demonstrated that it had no effect. Subjects in the 5-week study were male endurance cyclists.[198]

Dosage:

Tea, 100ml (1/3 cup) per day.
General use, 2-3 grams per day.

Fatigue

Having increased energy levels makes life easier, even if it's just to get through the day's responsibilities and work requirements. Chronic fatigue syndrome is separate from generalized fatigue. CFS is an illness that affects the entire body and needs treatment other than just rest.

Ganoderma lucidum [Reishi]

Researchers investigated a polysaccharide in G. lucidum called Ganopoly and its effectiveness in treating chronic fatigue syndrome. The 2005 study demonstrated that Ganopoly showed promise in treating chronic fatigue in human subjects.[199]

Dosage:

Tea, 100-200ml/day (3/4 cup).

Tincture, 2-3 droppers per day (2-3ml total) or for targeted use, 10ml 3x/day.

Dried or Fresh, 3-5 grams/day.

Ophiocordyceps sinensis [Cordyceps]

Intake of O. sinensis demonstrated increased energy in humans, likely due to the reduction of oxidative stress through scavenging oxygen free radicals.[200] [201]

Dosage:

Tea, 100ml (1/3 cup) per day.

General use, 2-3 grams per day.

Taiwanofungus camphoratus [Stout Camphor Fungus]

An extract of T. camphoratus claims to increase metabolism after exercise and decrease physiological fatigue. In 2008, a Taiwanese company received a US-patent to create this supplement.[202]

Dosage:

1-3 grams/day.

Fungal Diseases

Fungal diseases are caused by types of fungi or mushrooms and in this case, one mushroom shows promise in treating a few fungal diseases.

Pleurotus ostreatus [Oyster Mushroom]

P. ostreatus inhibited the growth of Trichophyton and Epidermophyton.[203]

Dosage:

Dried, 3-9 grams/day.
Fresh, 2-3 grams per day.
General use, 1-2 grams extract per day.

Gastrointestinal Issues

Our gastrointestinal health is related and significant to our overall health. If the gut is not working properly, it can cause a myriad of other health problems.

Agaricus bisporus [Button Mushroom]

A 2018 study into A. bisporus and its effects on gut health when compared with meat consumption demonstrated that there wasn't a lot of difference except in the amount of stool produced.[204]

A 2019 study involving pigs showed A. bisporus acted as a prebiotic, reduced inflammation, and shows promise for improving overall intestinal health.[205]

Dosage:

Eaten fresh, 4-8oz.

Hericium erinaceus [Lion's Mane]
Rats administered H. erinaceus orally were shown to have improved gastrointestinal function, specifically relating to the gastric mucus barrier which prevents gastric acid from entering the stomach.[206]

Dosage:
Tea, 100ml 2-3 times per day (1/3 cup).
Dried, 3-5 grams per day.

Ophiocordyceps sinensis [Cordyceps]
Extracts of O. sinensis have been shown to regulate intestinal bacteria and improve overall gut health. It did not kill or stop salmonella, E.coli, or lactobacillus bacteria, however, it did increase good bacteria levels.[207]

Dosage:
Tea, 100ml (1/3 cup) per day.
General use, 2-3 grams per day.

General Well-Being
Ophiocordyceps sinensis [Cordyceps]
Overall well-being was associated with regular intake of O. sinensis. This improvement was associated with properties of O. sinensis that reduced oxidative stress through the scavenging of oxygen free radical cells. Respiratory capacity was increased and memory loss, fatigue, tinnitus, dizziness, and intolerance to cold were all reduced.[208] (See also Endurance, Fatigue, and Immune System.)

Dosage:
Tea, 100ml (1/3 cup) per day.
General use, 2-3 grams per day.

Hearing Loss

There are many types of hearing loss and hearing loss can happen at any age. It can be age-related or due to genetic factors. Not many mushrooms have been studied in treating issues related to hearing loss, however, H. erinaceus shows good potential in improving one type.

Hericium erinaceus [Lion's Mane]

Sensorineural hearing loss occurs naturally due to age. It starts as an inability to hear higher-pitched sounds and then progresses to include more sounds. It is thought that Presbycusis, the most common type of Sensorinerual hearing loss, is a precursor to dementia and possibly Alzheimer's disease. Research shows that patients with this type of hearing loss have low nerve regeneration factors. Since H. erinaceus can regenerate nerves (see Nerve Regeneration), its use in treating hearing loss may be valuable. Mice tested showed slowed overall deterioration. [209]

Dosage:
For nerve damage, 3-5 grams per day.

Hemorrhaging

Excessive loss of blood due to a cut or wound can be life-threatening. Hemorrhaging can happen in all areas of the body.

Fomitopsis betulina [Birch Polypore]
Strips of raw, undoctored F. betulina applied externally to wounds or cuts have styptic abilities.[210]

Dosage:
General use, 1 teaspoon tincture twice a day.
Tea, 2-3 8oz cups per day (3-12 grams dried mushroom).

Panellus stipticus [Bitter Oyster Mushroom]
Used in traditional Chinese medicine, slivers or slices of this mushroom are used to stop bleeding.

Used to stop bleeding, apply fresh or dried.

Hepatitis B
A virus, HBV (hepatitis B virus), infects the body and causes inflammation of the liver. Some infections are temporary and will go away on their own. Other Hepatitis B infections do not get better and last a lifetime – called chronic HBV. A person suffering from chronic HBV often experiences severe issues of the liver, including cancer, cirrhosis (scarring), and liver failure. Some symptoms of HBV are jaundice, dark-colored urine, and pale bowel movements.

A few mushrooms show promise in improving liver function and reducing the side-effects of an HPV infection.

Agaricus subrufescens [Almond Mushroom]

A one-year study of patients with Hepatitis B demonstrated that A. subrufescens improves and normalizes liver function. There were four patients in the study and they took 1500mg of extract daily. It was shown not to cure Hepatitis B, though.[211]

In a later study, two patients with severe liver damage died after taking an extract of A. subrufescens, although it was not clear if the extract specifically caused the deaths.[212]

Dosage:
Eaten fresh, 4-8oz.

Ophiocordyceps sinensis [Cordyceps]
A significant reduction of the Hepatitis B viral load was observed with treatments of O. sinensis.[213]

Dosage:
Tea, 100ml (1/3 cup) per day.
General use, 2-3 grams per day.

Phellinus linteus [Black Hoof Mushroom]
In Chinese medicine, this fungus is commonly prescribed for hepatitis infections. Current research demonstrates the potential for protecting against liver fibrosis.[214]

Dosage:
Dried, 10-30 grams per day.
General use, 2-3 grams extract per day.

Taiwanofungus camphoratus [Stout Camphor Fungus]

Polysaccharides extracted from several strains of T. camphoratus exhibited anti-hepatitis B virus activity.[215]

Dosage:
1-3 grams/day.
For liver disease, 1-3 grams extract per day.

Hepatitis C

As with Hepatitis B, Hepatitis C is inflammation of the liver and is caused by a virus HCV (hepatitis C virus). It can last a few weeks or it can be a life-time chronic illness that seriously affects liver health.

Inonotus obliquus [Chaga]

Extracts of I. obliquus have demonstrated the ability to inhibit Hepatitis C viruses.[216]

Dosage:
Dried, 1/2 teaspoon per day (2.5oz).
Tincture, 2-3 droppers per day (2-3ml total).
Tea, 1-2 6oz cups per day.

High Cholesterol

Cholesterol occurs naturally in the body and the correct amount we need is manufactured within us. Our diets often introduce additional amounts of cholesterol into the body and we become overloaded. The cholesterol combines with other substances in our blood and forms plaque, which builds up in the arteries and leads to heart attacks, stroke, diabetes, and other serious issues.

High cholesterol is becoming a common diagnosis and there are quite a few drugs available to reduce cholesterol levels. Many of these have very serious side-effects and can cause long-term damage to internal organs. Developing a natural cholesterol-reducer without the side-effects is extremely important, as well as adjusting our diet and exercise to reduce plaque build-up. Many mushrooms show great potential in alleviating or maintaining cholesterol levels.

Agaricus bisporus [Button Mushroom]
This mushroom contains natural levels of lovastatin, which is a drug prescribed for high cholesterol.[217]

Dosage:
Eaten fresh, 4-8oz.

Auricularia auricula-judae [Jelly Ear Fungus]
Extracts of A. auricula-judae have been shown in lab tests to reduce overall cholesterol.

In rats, these fungi were shown to reduce LDL (bad) cholesterol while preserving HDL (good) cholesterol.[218]

Dosage:
Eaten fresh, 1-2 oz.
General-use, 2-3 grams extract per day.

Flammulina velutipes [Enoki]
The rich dietary fiber in F. velutipes quickens the

decomposition of cholesterol and shows promise in reducing TG, TC, and LDL levels.[219]

Dosage:
Dried, 8-9 grams per day.
Fresh, 30-50 grams per day.

Inonotus obliquus [Chaga]
Studies show that I. obliquus can lower blood cholesterol levels as well as reduce glucose, triglycerides, and fatty acids.[220]

Dosage:
Dried, 1/2 teaspoon per day (2.5oz).
Tincture, 2-3 droppers per day (2-3ml total).
Tea, 1-2 6oz cups per day.

Laetiporus sulphureus [Chicken of the Woods]
In clinical trials, cholesterol was significantly lowered during a 4-week study. It worked as well as the drug lovastatin with no side effects.[221]

Dosage:
Fresh, 4-6 oz. per day.

Lentinula edodes [Shiitake]
Eritadenine, a component of L. edodes has demonstrated the ability to lower overall cholesterol levels. A 2013 study using mice showed that eritadenine may regulate lipid metabolism and that L. edodes shows promise in treating high cholesterol.[222]

Dosage:
For high cholesterol, 9-15 grams per day (fruiting body).

Ophiocordyceps sinensis [Cordyceps]
A 30-day treatment showed total cholesterol levels significantly decreased.[223]

Dosage:
Tea, 100ml (1/3 cup) per day.
General use, 2-3 grams per day.

Pleurotus ostreatus [Oyster Mushroom]
A 1996 study examined the effects of feeding powdered P. ostreatus versus the whole mushroom to rats with high cholesterol. After 12 weeks, serum cholesterol levels were reduced by 52% with the whole mushroom and by 33% with the powder. Cholesterol absorption was decreased by 16% with consumption of the whole mushroom while no change was shown with the extract.[224]

A 2003 study explored the effect of powdered P. ostreatus on lipid and plasma profiles in rats with high cholesterol. Their plasma total cholesterol was reduced by 28%, lipoprotein cholesterol was reduced by 55%, triglycerides were reduced by 34%, non-esterified fatty acid was reduced by 30%, and total liver cholesterol was reduced by 34%. This same formula given to rats with normal cholesterol levels did not show any effects.[225]

Lovastatin, a natural component of P. ostreatus and other fungi, is now used by pharmaceutical drug companies in formulas to treat high cholesterol. Lovastatin was first discovered and developed from Aspergillus terreus. P. ostreatus contains up to 2.8% lovastatin.[226] In 2016, there were over 11 million prescriptions for lovastatin in the USA.[227]

Dosage:
For high cholesterol, 15-20 grams per day (dried).

HIV

This disease destroys the white blood cells in your immune system that fight infection. There is no cure but there are drugs that can alleviate symptoms and allow a person to live with the disease for a long time. Research into mushrooms for treating symptoms, boosting the immune system, and preventing the infection is ongoing.

Fomitopsis betulina [Birch Polypore]
A unique betulinic acid found in F. betulina blocks virus replication in HIV. [228]
Dosage:
General use, 1 teaspoon tincture twice a day.
Tea, 2-3 8oz cups per day (3-12 grams dried mushroom).

Inonotus obliquus [Chaga]
The immunomodulation properties of I. obliquus have shown potential in combating HIV.[229]

Dosage:

Dried, 1/2 teaspoon per day (2.5oz).

Tincture, 2-3 droppers per day (2-3ml total).

Tea, 1-2 6oz cups per day.

Laetiporus sulphureus [Chicken of the Woods]

This mushroom demonstrated impressive results when lab-tested as a potential contender in the fight against HIV.[230]

Dosage:

Fresh, 4-6 oz. per day.

High Blood Pressure (Hypertension)

High blood pressure, hypertension, can lead to heart disease, stroke, and potentially death. Diets high in salt, fat, and/or cholesterol can lead to hypertension. Besides dietary changes, there are medications prescribed to treat hypertension. Several mushroom types are being investigated for treating hypertension in a more natural way and without serious side-effects.

Flammulina velutipes [Enoki]

A lab study done in 2007 showed F. velutipes may be good at treating hypertension.[231]

Dosage:

Dried, 8-9 grams per day.

Fresh, 30-50 grams per day.

Ganoderma lucidum [Reishi]

A study of G. lucidum extract in treating hypertension demonstrated that a 2-month regimen improved and reduced blood pressure.[232]

Dosage:
Tea, 100-200ml/day (3/4 cup).
Tincture, 2-3 droppers per day (2-3ml total) or for targeted use, 10ml 3x/day.
Dried or Fresh, 3-5 grams/day.

Pleurotus cornucopiae [Horn of Plenty Oyster]
A 2005 study with hypertensive rats demonstrated that a phytochemical, D-Mannitol, found naturally in P. cornucopiae, inhibits ACE (Angiotensin-converting enzyme). ACE is a major part of the system which controls blood pressure.[233]

Dosage:
For high cholesterol, 15-20 grams per day (dried).

Low Blood Pressure (Hypoglycemia)

Low blood sugar (or blood glucose) is caused when your liver attempts to release glucose for energy but it isn't working properly. It is often associated with diabetes and diabetes medications, however, that isn't always the case. Finding a cure with mushrooms that works well for diabetics and non-diabetics alike is a big area of study. See the Diabetes section for more information about studies involving blood glucose levels.

Auricularia auricula-judae [Jelly Ear Fungus]
An extract of A. auricula-judae impacted and lowered insulin, urinary glucose levels, and plasma glucose levels

in diabetic mice.[234]

Dosage:
Eaten fresh, 1-2 oz.
General-use, 2-3 grams extract per day.

Inonotus obliquus [Chaga]
A study with rats demonstrated that a fermented extract of I. obliquus had hypoglycemic effects.[235]

Dosage:
Dried, 1/2 teaspoon per day (2.5oz).
Tincture, 2-3 droppers per day (2-3ml total).
Tea, 1-2 6oz cups per day.

Immune System (including Autoimmune Disorders)

Layered defenses in the immune system protect us from infections. When a pathogen breaks through, the immune system responds in an immediate non-specific way to deal with it. When the non-specific response isn't adequate, the body activates the third layer, called the adaptive immune system.

When our bodies cannot handle the infection alone, immune-boosting drugs are prescribed to control the infection and bring the immune system back to normal. Sometimes, our adaptive immune system overreacts leading to autoimmune disorders and excessive inflammation. This also frequently happens in organ transplants as the body rejects the new organ.

Treatment with immunomodulators, or bidirectional

modulators, is of extreme interest since it means the immune system is boosted, activated, or restored as the body needs it. Immunomodulators possess anti-inflammatory actions as well as pro-inflammatory actions. There are multiple immunomodulatory drugs used by doctors currently, however, they have many undesirable side-effects, including nausea, vomiting, headaches, and diarrhea.

Immunomodulators are used to treat autoimmune disorders, such as Crohn's Disease, Rheumatoid arthritis, Multiple sclerosis, HIV, Lupus, Inflammatory Bowel Syndrome, Psoriasis, and Hashimoto's.

Coriolus versicolor [Turkey Tail]
PSP (a polysaccharopeptide) in C. versicolor shows immunomodulatory properties. In many Eastern cultures, it is widely accepted as an adjunct to cancer treatment.[236]

Dosage:
For immune support, 1-2 grams extract per day.

Flammulina velutipes [Enoki]
Lectin and beta-D-glucan are two active components of F. velutipes and are shown to balance the immune system.[237] [238] Additionally, the polysaccharides in F. velutipes possess immunomodulation abilities.[239]

Dosage:
Dried, 8-9 grams per day.
Fresh, 30-50 grams per day.

Ganoderma lucidum [Reishi]

A 2005 article discussed and researched the immunomodulatory effects of different mushrooms and determined that G. lucidum, along with others, contains properties that enhance the immune system.[240]

Dosage:
Tea, 100-200ml/day (3/4 cup).
Tincture, 2-3 droppers per day (2-3ml total) or for targeted use 10ml 3x/day.
Dried or Fresh, 3-5 grams/day.

Inonotus obliquus [Chaga]
The polysaccharide and exopolysaccharides in I. obliquus have been shown to possess immune modulation activity.[241]

Dosage:
Dried, 1/2 teaspoon per day (2.5oz).
Tincture, 2-3 droppers per day (2-3ml total).
Tea, 1-2 6oz cups per day.

Lentinula edodes [Shiitake]
A study of healthy adults taking whole, dried L. edodes demonstrated that daily consumption improved immunity.[242]

Dosage:
For immune support, 2-6 grams extract per day.

Lignosus rhinocerus [Tiger's Milk]
Several studies have shown the immunomodulatory properties of L. rhinocerus extracts.[243]

Dosage:
General use, 250-500 mg/day.

Phellinus linteus [Black Hoof Mushroom]

Studies done on extracts of P. linteus demonstrate they have strong immune-boosting and immunomodulation properties.[244]

Dosage:
Dried, 10-30 grams per day.
General use, 2-3 grams extract per day.

Ophiocordyceps sinensis [Cordyceps]

A human trial in 2019 showed O. sinensis extract improved the overall immune-system in healthy adults after taking it for 8 weeks. [245]

Research demonstrates O. sinensis operates as a bidirectional modulator of the immune system, which means it both improves and suppresses it as needed. This indicates O. sinensis has the potential for treating autoimmune diseases and for use as an immunosuppressant after organ transplant.[246]

Dosage:
Tea, 100ml (1/3 cup) per day.
General use, 2-3 grams per day.

Taiwanofungus camphoratus [Stout Camphor Fungus]

A 2018 study verified the potential immunomodulatory properties of T. camphoratus extracts in an 8-week

study with mice.[247]
Dosage:
1-3 grams/day.

Tricholoma matsutake [Matsutake]

An isolated polysaccharide in T. matsutake demonstrated a broad range of immune-boosting activities.[248]

Dosage:
Fresh or dried, 4-8 oz. /per day.

Inflammation

The causes of inflammation are many, as are the treatments. Long-term inflammation can lead to the development of inflammatory diseases. There are plenty of treatments on the market today, from topical over-the-counter creams to steroid-based drugs. The issue with many of the current medications is that they have undesirable, and often serious, side effects. Some of these side effects are stroke, gastrointestinal issues, gastritis, renal issues, and heart attack. There has been much research into the use of mushrooms as safe treatments for inflammation, specifically, the studies focus on efficacy and absence of side effects.

Agaricus subrufescens [Almond Mushroom]

General anti-inflammatory agents were found in studies of A. subrufescens.[249]

Dosage:
Eaten fresh, 4-8oz.

Auricularia auricula-judae [Jelly Ear Fungus]

Polysaccharides in A. auricula-judae demonstrated significant anti-inflammatory properties when tested on rats with edema. [250]

In a study done on acute lung injuries, this mushroom reduced inflammation and improved the effects of the injury in rats.[251]

Dosage:
Eaten fresh, 1-2 oz.
General-use, 2-3 grams extract per day.

Flammulina velutipes [Enoki]
A 2014 study of anti-inflammatory actions of 5 mushrooms (Agaricus bisporus – white and brown, Lentinus edodes, F. velutipes, and Pleurotus ostreatus), it was discovered that F. velutipes along with L. edodes and P. ostreatus, were the best at treating inflammation. This study also showed that cooking the mushrooms deceased the anti-inflammatory action. Tests need to be conducted as to what heat level is ideal to maintain medicinal properties while still cooking the mushroom so it is safe to eat.[252]

Dosage:
Dried, 8-9 grams per day.
Fresh, 30-50 grams per day.

Fomitopsis betulina [Birch Polypore]
The triterpenoids in F. betulina contain many anti-inflammatory properties. In a test on rats with minor burns, the results were better than using cortisone. [253]

Dosage:
General use, 1 teaspoon tincture twice a day.
Tea, 2-3 8oz cups per day (3-12 grams dried mushroom).

Fomitopsis pincola [Red-Banded Polypore]

A small study investigating the triterpenoids in F. pincola showed promise as an anti-inflammatory. Specifically, an extract reduced swelling in the ears of mice.[254]

Dosage:
General use, 20-30 grams twice daily.

Hericium erinaceus [Lion's Mane]

A 14-day study of rats showed reduced edema in the stomach, specifically relating to gastric ulcers and gastrointestinal health.[255] In a lab study to test the effects of H. erinaceus on low-grade inflammation of fat tissues, a potential factor of metabolic diseases like heart disease and diabetes, the extract showed promising results. Inflammation of the fat tissue was decreased and potentially could be prevented.[256]

Dosage:
For gastric ulcer, 25-50 grams day (fruiting body).

Laetiporus sulphureus [Chicken of the Woods]

The exopolysaccharide (EPS) found in L. sulphureus is shown to inhibit inflammatory responses.[257] Specifically, the anti-inflammatory actions in microglial cells are important because those cells are vital for maintaining the health of the central nervous system. Uncontrolled microglial cells damage neurons and may be a contributing factor to the development of Parkinson's and Alzheimer's.

Dosage:
Fresh, 4-6 oz. per day.

Lentulina edodes [Shiitake]
(See study report under Flammulina velutipes.)

Dosage:
Fresh, 3-5 oz. /day.
Dried, 2-6 grams/day.

Lignosus rhinocerus [Tiger's Milk]
During research, an extract of L. rhinocerus was tested on rats and showed remarkable anti-inflammatory action.[258]

Dosage:
General use, 250-500 mg/day.

Phellinus linteus [Black Hoof Mushroom]
Several studies have shown P. linteus has great potential for treating inflammation, including inflammatory diseases and acute injuries that include inflammation.[259]
Dosage:
For rheumatoid arthritis, 3 grams extract per day.

Pleurotus ostreatus [Oyster Mushroom]

(See study report under Flammulina velutipes.)

Dosage:
Dried, 3-9 grams/day.
Fresh, 2-3 grams per day.
General use, 1-2 grams extract per day.

Insomnia

Sleep is a necessary part of life and anyone who struggles to get quality rest understands the cascading negative effects this can have on one's life. Not many mushrooms have been studied for treating insomnia, however, G. lucidum does look promising.

Ganoderma lucidum [Reishi]

An extract of G. lucidum was tested for its use for treating sleep issues in rats. Results showed the extract prolonged sleep.[260]

Dosage:
For insomnia, 1-3 grams extract per day.

Irritable Bowel Syndrome (IBS)

A disease of the large intestine, IBS (or IBD) causes bloating, cramping, constipation and/or diarrhea. It doesn't harm the intestines but it does cause a lot of discomfort and pain. There is no known cause or cure, the best that can be done is to treat the symptoms and attempt to alleviate them. Diet management, stress management, and medications are used for this purpose. The use of mushrooms to decrease inflammation and sensitivity in the intestinal tract may be useful in treating IBS.

Grifola frondosa [Hen of the Woods]

In a 2010 study researching the efficacy of G. frondosa in alleviating bowel inflammation, it was discovered that an extract of G. frondosa could reduce inflammation and be a potential treatment for IBD/IBS.[261]

Dosage:
Fresh, 3-7 grams/day or more.

Hericium erinaceus [Lion's Mane]

Extracts of H. erinaceus were administered to mice to test for the reduction of acute intestinal inflammation. The extract suppressed inflammatory responses, protected the mucus membranes surrounding internal organs, and improved colitis.[262]

A study of ulcers in rats demonstrated increased gastrointestinal health and reduction of ulcer symptoms. The gastro mucus barrier, which separates gastric acid from the stomach, improved significantly. Additionally, swelling of the stomach was significantly reduced.[263]

Dosage:
Tea, 100ml 2-3 times per day (1/3 cup).
Dried, 3-5 grams per day.

Kidney Function

Kidneys are responsible for removing waste and water from our bodies. Improperly functioning kidneys or kidney disease is a serious issue.

Ophiocordyceps sinensis [Cordyceps]

A review of O. sinensis use in conjunction with kidney transplants demonstrated it improved graft function and potentially reduced rejection. It did not show any effect on patient survival.[264]

Dosage:

For kidney function, 3 grams per day.

Lesions

Lesions happen when the tissue of an organism experiences damage or an abnormal change. They can occur anywhere on the body, internally and externally. Some lesions are cancerous while others are benign. Research into lesions usually focuses on a specific type since there are so many and they are so varied.

Pleurotus ostreatus [Oyster Mushroom]

In a study on the effects of pleuran (a polysaccharide found in P. ostreatus) on rats with colon lesions found it to reduce the development of lesions by more than 50%.[265]

Dosage:

Dried, 3-9 grams/day.
Fresh, 2-3 grams per day.
General use, 1-2 grams extract per day.

Libido

Low libido can be caused by age, medical conditions, or genetic issues. People experiencing reduced libido can often rectify this with changes to diet or exercise, however, that doesn't work for everyone.

Ophiocordyceps sinensis [Cordyceps]
Treatments with O. sinensis demonstrated increased libido in females and males.[266] [267]

O. sinensis is often referred to as a Himalayan Viagra due to it growing naturally in the region and the claims of local people as to its ability to enhance vigor and vitality.[268]

Dosage:
For libido, 3 grams per day.

Liver Disease
There are many drugs on the market to treat liver disease. Unfortunately, many of these have side effects that cause other dangerous diseases.

Flammulina velutipes [Enoki]
Preliminary studies show F. velutipes may prevent, and possibly cure, liver disease.[269]
Dosage:
Dried, 8-9 grams per day.
Fresh, 30-50 grams per day.

Ganoderma lucidum [Reishi]
In a 2008 study of rats and hepatic fibrosis (a symptom of liver disease), an extract of G. lucidum showed

potential in treating this fibrosis and possibly preventing it.[270]

Dosage:
Tea, 100-200ml/day (3/4 cup).
Tincture, 2-3 droppers per day (2-3ml total) or for targeted use 10ml 3x/day.
Dried or Fresh, 3-5 grams/day.

Laetiporus sulphureus [Chicken of the Woods]
Eburicoic acid, the main bioactive element in L. sulphureus, combined with trametenolic acid B, also from L. sulphureus demonstrated the ability to reduce liver cell damage in rats. It also reduced instances of liver fibrosis.[271]

Dosage:
Fresh, 4-6 oz. per day.

Lignosus rhinocerus [Tiger's Milk]
A study conducted on obese hamsters administered L. rhinocerus showed improved liver health and reduced disease symptoms.[272]

Dosage:
General use, 250-500 mg/day.

Taiwanofungus camphoratus [Stout Camphor Fungus]
A study in 2015 demonstrated T. camphoratus has significant potential in treating liver cancer. Specifically,

it shows promise as an adjunct therapy in combination with chemotherapy.[273]

Dosage:
For liver disease, 1-3 grams extract per day.

Malaria

Compounding the devastation caused by this disease, there are now many drugs that are ineffectual because the parasites are becoming increasingly resistant. (Also see Antimicrobial.)

Agaricus subrufescens [Almond Mushroom]
Mice treated with an extract of A. subrufescens in a 2015 study showed increased survival, reduced weight loss, lower parasitization, and reduced occurrence of cerebral malaria.[274]

Dosage:
Eaten fresh, 4-8oz.

Laetiporus sulphureus [Chicken of the Woods]
Extracts of L. sulphureus showed promise as agents to fight the strain of malaria, Plasmodium falciparum, which is the severest strain of malaria and implicated in the majority of malaria deaths. [275]

Dosage:
Fresh, 4-6 oz. per day.

Memory

Memory issues can occur due to age or disease-related trauma. Even people without obvious memory issues should consider taking proactive steps to improve memory before it becomes an issue. Memory-related issues can also cause depression and anxiety, especially in older folks. H. erinaceus has demonstrated great potential in improving memory in healthy as well as memory-impaired adults.

Hericium erinaceus [Lion's Mane]

Oral doses of H. erinaceus were given to mice for two months and the mice demonstrated improved recognition memory. Recognition memory is the ability to differentiate between familiar and novel experiences. It is important cognitively, for general memory function, and physiologically as it affects overall well-being. Reduced novelty-seeking is associated with anxiety, depression, and inability to cope. In these tests, the mice sought out new novel experiences. The mice seeking out novel experiences shows promise for future studies with H. erinaceus treating depression and anxiety, as well as improving overall memory function.[276]

Mice administered a dose of H. erinaceus for 2 months showed improved locomotor activity (motor function), yet no improvement in spatial memory.[277]

Dosage:
Tea, 100ml 2-3 times per day (1/3 cup).
Dried, 3-5 grams per day.

Menopause

Menopause can cause a wide variety of symptoms, many of them disruptive to everyday life. Reducing or alleviating the symptoms can help a lot of women who are struggling, especially when the symptoms last for years. Preliminary studies of menopausal women using H. erinaceus are very promising.

Hericium erinaceus [Lion's Mane]

Menopausal women were given 2 grams of H. erinaceus over 4 weeks and demonstrated fewer symptoms of depression and anxiety. Specifically, concentration, irritation, and anxiety categories showed improvement.[278]

Dosage:

Tea, 100ml 2-3 times per day (1/3 cup).
Dried, 3-5 grams per day.

Myocardial Ischemia-Reperfusion (IR)

After a heart attack, blood flow needs to be restored to the arteries that were blocked. The act of restoring blood flow often causes tissue damage due to a lack of oxygen (ischemia). IR injuries can result in stroke and brain injuries as well as the failure of sores, ulcers, and wounds to heal. IR is a common injury in cardiac arrest, affecting a large portion of the population, and is becoming a common cause of death.

Cyclosporine is the common treatment for IR though it doesn't always work. Other treatments are also being investigated to reduce inflammation and prevent cell death.

Phellinus linteus [Black Hoof Mushroom]

A 2017 study on rats demonstrated the potential for a P. linteus extracts to treat IR. Myocardial (heart) injury was reduced due to lessened obstruction of blood flow to the organ.[279]

Dosage:
Dried, 10-30 grams per day.
General use, 2-3 grams extract per day.

Nerve Regeneration

The nervous system is a complex and delicate structure that includes the brain, spinal, and peripheral nerves. Injuries can occur due to trauma or disease. Many progressive diseases, like Alzheimer's, Parkinson's, and multiple sclerosis induce progressive deterioration.

Hericium erinaceus [Lion's Mane]

A liquid extract of H. erinaceus was given to injured mice for 14 days. The nerves regenerated better with the treatment. Additionally, the treatment improved motor function recovery. Mice being treated with H. erinaceus improved 4-7 days quicker than non-H. erinaceus treated subjects.

The recommended dosage for nerve regeneration is 3-5 grams of powdered H. erinaceus per day.[280]

Dosage:
For nerve damage, 3-5 grams per day.

Lignosus rhinocerus [Tiger's Milk]

An extract of the sclerotium ("root" of the fungi) was lab tested for potential nerve regeneration actions. Results demonstrated that the extract affected neurite growth and proved that it contained neuroactive compounds.[281]

Dosage:
General use, 250-500 mg/day.

Neurodegenerative Diseases

Alzheimer's, Parkinson's, and Huntington's disease are just a few of the neurodegenerative diseases that afflict the population, the majority of them occurring with increased age. These diseases impair movement, balance, talking, and breathing. The cause can be genetic, due to a medical condition, a stroke, chemical or toxin-related, from a virus, or in some cases, unknown. The majority have no cure and treatments focus on relieving pain, increasing mobility, and improving overall symptoms.

Flammulina velutipes [Enoki]

A lab study testing the properties of F. velutipes extracts discovered the potential for enhancing learning and cognitive abilities.[282]

In 2015, an extract of F. velutipes was demonstrated to improve spatial search behavior in rats as well as work against the progression of memory and learning impairments.[283]

A 2017 study of mice demonstrated the scope of F.

velutipes in improving cognitive abilities. It also discovered a possible mechanism for suppressing neuroinflammation (inflammation of the nervous tissue).[284]

Dosage:
For neurodegenerative issues, 3-5 grams per day.

Phellinus linteus [Black Hoof Mushroom]
Preliminary lab studies demonstrate the potential for P. linteus in treating, and possibly preventing neurodegenerative diseases.[285]

Dosage:
Dried, 10-30 grams per day.
General use, 2-3 grams extract per day.

Neuropathy

Due to disease or trauma, nerves are damaged and stop functioning properly. One of the main causes is diabetes and is called diabetic neuropathy. Symptoms include numbness, tingling, burning sensations, shooting pain, urinary issues, and dizziness. Current treatments include diet changes, pain management, and medication. As incidences of diabetes increase, so too do studies to reverse or manage symptoms.

Hericium erinaceus [Lion's Mane]
A study of rats with diabetic neuropathy showed significant pain relief after 6 weeks of treatment. Additionally, the antioxidant activity of the H. erinaceus extract improved the overall diabetic state.[286]

Dosage:
For nerve damage, 3-5 grams per day.

Obesity

There are hundreds of medicines, supplements, and "miracle cures" on the market today to combat obesity. The efficacy of most are incidental, to say the least, but it doesn't stop the multi-million dollar industry from creating more. There haven't been many studies of mushrooms and obesity, however, L. rhinocerus does show promise as a potential adjunct to weight-loss.

Lignosus rhinocerus [Tiger's Milk]
In a 2014 study of obese hamsters, an extract of L. rhinocerus improved health and inhibited weight gain. [287]

Dosage:
General use, 250-500 mg/day.

Parasites

A parasite is an organism that lives within another organism. Many parasites affect humans and lead to sickness, severe illness, and even death. Some pass on diseases that can be fatal. Most parasites need specific treatments; there is no one cure-all for a wide variety of types.

Agaricus subrufescens [Almond Mushroom]
An extract of A. subrufescens was tested in a treatment

for Leishmaniasis, which is a tropical disease transmitted by a parasite carried by the sandfly. This disease can cause ulcers and even death. Current treatments are expensive and have undesirable side-effects.

Mice treated with the A. subrufescens extract demonstrated a 60% reduction in inflammation and reduced parasite burden to the lymph nodes, spleen, and liver.[288]

Dosage:
Eaten fresh, 4-8oz.

Parkinson's

A neurodegenerative disease that progressively gets worse, Parkinson's has no cure. The cause isn't entirely known either – it can sometimes be genetic but not always. Environmental factors and exposure to chemicals are a potential origination. Parkinson's is onset by the brain not producing enough dopamine. It is difficult to diagnose and treatment is focused entirely on alleviating symptoms. H. erinaceus studies show a potentially viable treatment.

Hericium erinaceus [Lion's Mane]
A low-dose of H. erinaceas given to mice for 25 days showed improvement in oxidative stress, which is an imbalance of antioxidants and free radicals in the body. There were also fewer lesions in the brain caused by the loss of dopamine. [289]

Dosage:
For nerve damage, 3-5 grams per day.

Pulmonary Diseases

Diseases of the lung are varied and often life-threatening. COPD, influenza, pneumonia, tuberculosis, lung cancer, and asthma are a few that affect our lungs and lead to respiratory issues and failure. Lung disease is currently the #3 killer in the United States. Treatments range from surgery and medications, to lifestyle changes. F. officinalis has shown potential in treating a couple of diseases of the lungs.

Fomitopsis officinalis [Agarikon]

Research indicates F. officinalis shows great potential in targeting specific infections, like tuberculosis or pseudotuberculosis.[290]

Dosage:
General use, 20-30 grams twice daily.

Purgative

A laxative is needed for a variety of reasons. Before the advent of current eastern medicine, purgatives were prescribed for all manner of issues, in the belief that the body needed to expel whatever was ailing it. Purgatives are still used today, for treating severe constipation. Most purgatives have side effects, including cramps, flatulence, bloating, and headaches.

Fomitopsis betulina [Birch Polypore]

Traditional healers used extracts or concoctions infused with F. betulina as a purgative.

Dosage:
General use, 1 teaspoon tincture twice a day.
Tea, 2-3 8oz cups per day (3-12 grams dried mushroom).

Respiratory Issues

Respiratory issues can be simply bothersome, like a mild seasonal allergy, or life-altering and life-threatening, like respiratory failure. Treating respiratory issues before they become problematic is important. Several mushrooms show promise in alleviating respiratory issues, including asthma and bronchitis.

Ganoderma lucidum [Reishi]
(See Allergies section.)

Dosage:
For allergies, 500mg extract 3x/day.
For asthma, 1-3 grams extract per day.

Ophiocordyceps sinensis [Cordyceps]
An animal-based study demonstrated O. sinensis calmed coughs while increasing respiratory secretions to further expectoration. In guinea pigs, it is anti-asthmatic. Extracts of O. sinensis have been used to treat bronchial asthma and chronic bronchitis with good results.[291]

Dosage:
Tea, 100ml (1/3 cup) per day.

General use, 2-3 grams per day.

Pleurotus ostreatus [Oyster Mushroom]

A 2014 study of children with Recurrent Respiratory Tract Infections (RRTI) showed a treatment including pleuran, a polysaccharide found in P. ostreatus, reduced allergic reactions, and showed promise as a complementary treatment for this disease.[292]

Dosage:

Dried, 3-9 grams/day.

Fresh, 2-3 grams per day.

Skin Care

The skin is the largest human organ and needs care as much as our internal organs. It retains fluids, prevents dehydration, maintains even body temperature, and keeps harmful microbes away. All too often, we neglect our skin, taking its service for granted. Skin needs protection from the sun, from allergy sources, and much more. A couple of mushroom types are being studied for their use in protecting from these agitators.

Fomitopsis betulina [Birch Polypore]

Preliminary studies show F. betulina has promise in skincare treatments. In a lab study, UV-damage to skin was diminished.[293]

Dosage:

General use, 1 teaspoon tincture twice a day.

Tea, 2-3 8oz cups per day (3-12 grams dried mushroom).

Fomitopsis pinicola [Red-banded Polypore]

Studies show this polypore has anti-histamine properties as well as moisturizing and stimulating attributes.[294]

Dosage:
General use, 20-30 grams twice daily.

Stamina

Not just for endurance athletes, increased stamina also helps those with low energy due to illness, disease, or life-style.

Ophiocordyceps sinensis [Cordyceps]
(See entries under Fatigue & Endurance & Libido.)

Dosage:
Tea, 100ml (1/3 cup) per day.
General use, 2-3 grams per day.
For libido, 3 grams per day.

Staph Infection

Laetiporus sulphureus [Chicken of the Woods]
(See Antimicrobial.)

Dosage:
Fresh, 4-6 oz. per day.

Strength

Everyone wants increased strength, though not always for the same reasons. For athletes, it will allow longer training and better performance. For those with illnesses, expanded strength will decrease healing times and allow for better daily function. H. erinaceus has been used for hundreds of years to improve overall strength.

Hericium erinaceus [Lion's Mane]

In traditional Chinese medicine, H. erinaceus is used to fortify the five internal organs: liver, lung, spleen, heart, and kidney. These are vital to Qi, life force, and invigorating them brings enhanced strength to the body.[295]

Dosage:

Tea, 100ml 2-3 times per day (1/3 cup).
Dried, 3-5 grams per day.

Testosterone

Low testosterone affects libido and sperm production, however, it is also responsible for a host of other issues. Muscle mass, hair production (facial and body), and overall bone health are all related to testosterone levels. Men afflicted with low testosterone can take testosterone replacement therapy via injections, gel patches, or tablets. All of these options have risks and side-effects which include increased risk for prostate cancer and breast cancer. Mushroom studies with O. sinensis show excellent potential in treating low testosterone more naturally with reduced dangerous side-effects.

Ophiocordyceps sinensis [Cordyceps]

A 2004 study of the effects of O. sinensis on testosterone levels in mice demonstrated increased testosterone production in both immature and mature mice.[296]

Dosage:
For libido, 3 grams per day.

Tick-Borne Encephalitis (TBE)

Tick-borne diseases are on the rise worldwide and all of them are life-altering, if not life-threatening. The majority of people, including many doctors, struggle to get a correct diagnosis as tick-borne diseases are difficult to pinpoint. Treatments for these diseases and their myriad of symptoms are overwhelming and have as many side-effects as they do symptoms they alleviate.

Fomitopsis betulina [Birch Polypore]

A study exposing mice to TBE showed an extract of F. betulina had strong protective properties.[297]

Dosage:
General use, 1 teaspoon tincture twice a day.
Tea, 2-3 8oz cups per day (3-12 grams dried mushroom).

Tuberculosis

Fomitopsis officinalis [Agarikon]

(See Pulmonary.)

Dosage:
General use, 10-20 grams per day.

Tumors

The majority of tumors are related to a type of cancer, though many are also benign. Fighting tumor-causing cells is important in the fight to cure or alleviate cancer symptoms. For additional research into mushrooms and their usefulness in treating tumors, see the section on Cancer.

Agaricus subrufescens [Almond Mushroom]
(See Cancer entry.)

Dosage:
For cancer, 3 grams per day.

Auricularia auricula-judae [Jelly Ear Fungus]
Numerous studies have demonstrated the antitumor activities of A. auricula-judae.[298]

Dosage:
Eaten fresh, 1-2 oz.
General-use, 2-3 grams extract per day.

Fomitopsis betulina [Birch Polypore]
In a 1957 study of dogs with vaginal tumors, an extract of F. betulina was administered orally. The tumors disappeared after five weeks.[299]

Dosage:

General use, 1 teaspoon tincture twice a day.
Tea, 2-3 8oz cups per day (3-12 grams dried mushroom).

Grifola frondosa [Hen of the Woods]
In a 2017 study of tumors in mice, extracts of G. frondosa were found to stimulate antitumor responses.[300]

Dosage:
Fresh, 3-7 grams/day or more.

Inonotuus obliquus [Chaga]
Extracts of I. obliquus have shown effectiveness in fighting cervical, colon, leukemia, and liver tumors.[301]

Dosage:
Dried, 1/2 teaspoon per day (2.5oz).
Tincture, 2-3 droppers per day (2-3ml total).
Tea, 1-2 6oz cups per day.

Lentinula edodes [Shiitake]
A natural component of L. edodes, lentinan, was shown in a 2015 study to inhibit cell proliferation in bladder cancer patients in combination with regular chemotherapy treatment (with the drug gemcitabine). The results were better than with treatments solely with chemotherapy.[302]

Dosage:
Fresh, 3-5 oz. /day.
Dried, 2-6 grams/day.

Pleurotus ostreatus [Oyster Mushroom]
An element of P. ostreatus was tested and showed potential in causing cell death in tumors.[303]

Dosage:
Dried, 3-9 grams/day.
Fresh, 2-3 grams per day.
General use, 1-2 grams extract per day.

Ulcers
An ulcer is a slow-healing sore and it can be internal or external. They are very common, especially gastric (peptic) ulcers. While some will heal on their own, others require treatment with medicine or surgery. Gastric ulcers do not go away even when they are not symptomatic. Painfulness can be alleviated by not eating foods that irritate them, however, that is just a temporary fix. There is lots of promising research being done with mushrooms regarding gastric ulcers, especially with H. erinaceus.

Laetiporus sulphureus [Chicken of the Woods]
Oral administration of eburicoic acid, the main bioactive element of L. sulphureus, protected against gastric ulcers in lab studies.[304]

Dosage:
Fresh, 4-6 oz. per day.

Hericium erinaceus [Lion's Mane]
Extracts of H. erinaceus administered to rats showed

improved gastroprotection, specifically with the gastro mucus barrier. The gastro mucus barrier is the part of the stomach that contains gastric acid needed for digestion. Breaks in the barrier result in ulcers and damage to the stomach. A strong gastro mucus barrier indicates a protected digestive system and a decreased chance of ulcers. Decreased inflammation was also noted. The results were dose-dependent and were best at the highest dose of 400mg.[305]

Dosage:
For gastric ulcer, 25-50 grams day (fruiting body).

Urinary Tract

A healthy urinary tract is vital to life. The urinary tract drains toxins from the body. Urinary tract infections in women are the second most common infection in the body.

Ganoderma lucidum [Reishi]
Men suffering from lower urinary tract symptoms (LUTS) were treated with an extract of G. lucidum to test its effects. Results showed improvement in overall symptoms.

Dosage:
The recommended dose for men with this condition is 6mg/day.[306]

Vigor

Vigor includes strength as well as good health. All people should enjoy good vigor; it improves the enjoyment of life and the ability to embrace tasks and challenges.

Hericium erinaceus [Lion's Mane]

H. erinaceus is used in Chinese medicine to fortify the five internal organs: liver, lung, spleen, heart, and kidney. Strengthening the organs improves vigor and enhances overall health.[307]

Dosage:

Tea, 100ml 2-3 times per day (1/3 cup).
Dried, 3-5 grams per day.

Viruses

A virus creates an infection of the cells which replicates and can cause general unwellness, severe illness, or death. There are hundreds of viruses and they infect humans, animals, plants, and bacteria. Because of the broad scope, the treatments are generally specialized to a particular one. Several mushrooms are being researched to combat specific viruses with great potential.

The section Antimicrobial also deals with infections.

Fomitopsis betulina [Birch Polypore]

Studies show a betulinic acid (named YI-FH 312) blocks virus replications. Encephalitis infections were incapacitated. Yellow fever, the flu virus, and West Nile virus were all affected by the extract of F. betulina. [308]

Dosage:

General use, 1 teaspoon tincture twice a day.
Tea, 2-3 8oz cups per day (3-12 grams dried

166

mushroom).

Lignosus rhinocerus [Tiger's Milk]

A study of L. rhinocerus concerning dengue fever showed it has potential in treating this virus.[309]

Dosage:

General use, 250-500 mg/day.

Phellinus linteus [Black Hoof Mushroom]

Many studies on the antimicrobial activities of P. linteus demonstrate its potential in combating viral infections.[310]

Dosage:

Dried, 10-30 grams per day.

General use, 2-3 grams extract per day.

Pleurotus ostreatus [Oyster Mushroom]

An anti-viral protein called ubiquitin was isolated from P. ostreatus. Polysaccharides with immunomodulation effects have also been determined.[311]

Dosage:

Dried, 3-9 grams/day.

Fresh, 2-3 grams per day.

General use, 1-2 grams extract per day.

Pleurotus tuber-regium [Tuber Oyster Mushroom]

Glucans found in the sclerotia (the tuber) showed efficacy in a lab experiment treating Herpes type-1 and type-2.[312]

Dosage:
Dried, 3-9 grams/day.
Fresh, 2-3 grams per day.
General use, 1-2 grams extract per day.

Wounds

Small wounds aren't generally life-threatening, though if not cared for appropriately, they can become infected and spread. Treating them quickly is a key factor in preventing infection. F. betulina, in particular, is a wound treatment that has stood the test of time and shown its invaluable nature.

Fomitopsis betulina [Birch Polypore]

For hundreds (possibly thousands) of years, F. betulina was peeled or sliced and applied to wounds as an antiseptic and to stop bleeding. More recent studies show its efficacy as an antibiotic and antimicrobial.[313]

Hericium erinaceus [Lion's Mane]

In a study on rats, an extract of H. erinaceus was applied topically to wounds to measure healing time and scarring. The rats treated with the extract demonstrated faster healing with less scar tissue than those in the control group.[314]

Dosage:
Tea, 100ml 2-3 times per day (1/3 cup).
Dried, 3-5 grams per day.

CHAPTER 7

PREPARING MUSHROOMS AS MEDICINALS

There are several methods for ingesting mushrooms to experience their medicinal benefits. Usually, the best method depends on the type of mushroom. Many mushrooms simply aren't edible while others are quite tasty and can be included regularly in cooked dishes.

There is no best method for preparing mushrooms. Much depends on which medicinal property is desired and the type of mushroom. Also, the concentration desired plays a role in how best to prepare the mushroom. If the mushroom is being used to combat a specific disease or issue, an extract or tincture is best. If the mushroom is being used as a supplement for general health, eating it fresh is a popular option. For the best medicinal value, a dual extraction is recommended.

Dragon Images/Shutterstock.com

Quick Reference:

Extracts access polysaccharides, which enhance the immune system and provide antioxidants. Tinctures access terpenes (triterpenoids), which stabilize blood pressure, cholesterol, and boost anti-inflammatory response.

Water Extractions

The majority of research studies on the medicinal properties of mushrooms use a water extraction as the test-base. An extraction is the most popular method because it breaks down the cell walls of the mushroom and accesses the polysaccharides inside the cells. The polysaccharides are usually what carry the medicinal properties and a water extract increases bioavailability. Bioavailability refers to how easily the product can be absorbed and used by the body. An extract also increases the concentration of medicinal properties meaning much less needs to be consumed, as compared to eating whole mushrooms.

There have been studies recently assessing the usefulness of hot water extractions vs. cold water extractions. Hot water extractions are the most common because it is so similar to making a basic tea and is the method most often used by traditional practitioners. It is also widely believed that heat is needed to extract certain benefits from the mushroom.

One study done in 2016 demonstrated that a cold water extraction of a Pleurotus sp. provided higher bioavailability of antioxidants.[315] The cold-water process may not provide higher benefits with all mushrooms; this is still being researched and tested.

Best mushrooms for Water Extractions: Turkey Tail, Lion's Mane, Cordyceps, Shiitake, and Maitake.

Hot Water Extractions

As the name suggests, hot water is used to heat the raw mushrooms and extract the desired properties. The water temperature ranges from 175-350F (80-170C) and the heating time can vary as well.

An extract can include one mushroom or several mushroom types to combine benefits.

Hot Water Extraction, Basic Method

1. Combine 2-3 oz. dried mushrooms to 4 cups (1 liter) boiling water.

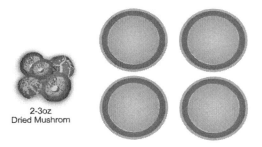

2-3oz
Dried Mushrom

2. Boil for 5 minutes.

3. Reduce heat and simmer for 1 hour.

4. Strain and reserve liquid.

5. Serve as tea, add to smoothies, coffee, or soup.

Cold/Hot Water Extraction, Method 2

1. In a pot, combine pieces of mushroom and cold water.

2. Let it soak for an hour.

3. Heat the water slowly until it reaches 165F (75C). Do not boil.

4. Turn off heat and steep for 1 hour.

5. The extract will be very dark.
6. Strain out the solid matter and throw away or save to be reused.

7. Enjoy hot or cold.
8. The mushroom pieces may be re-steeped multiple times, until the extract is no longer flavorful or dark in color.

Tinctures

Tinctures have two purposes. They are used to draw out the properties of mushrooms that cannot be eaten fresh, and they are used to concentrate the properties into focused serums. Tinctures are alcohol or glycerin-based and there are a variety of formulas for attaining the highest benefits. Alcohol-based tinctures bring out the triterpenoid components in mushrooms.

Alcohol breaks down polysaccharides and is not a recommended method if those are the mushroom components you are seeking. A double-extraction is better if you want the polysaccharides and triterpenoids.

<u>Best mushrooms for Tinctures:</u> Reishi, Chaga, Turkey Tail.

Kungtalon/Shutterstock.com

Alcohol-Based Tincture (Method 1 – dried mushrooms)

1. Cut up, break apart, grind or powder dry mushrooms. Depending on the type of mushroom, you may need some powerful appliances or muscles. Breaking them up increases the surface area, making a more thorough extraction.

2. Fill a quart-sized glass jar 3/4-ways with the dried mushrooms (dried mushrooms expand and need room to do so).

3. Add minimum 80-proof alcohol, leaving a few inches free at the top.

4. Close the jar lid tightly.

5. Store in a cool, dark location for 21-30 days. *Shake the jar daily.*

6. Strain out the solids.

7. Store in a jar in a cool, dark location.

Alcohol-Based Tincture (Method 2 – fresh mushrooms)

1. Cut fresh mushrooms into thin slices and combine them with 95% alcohol in a 1:5 ratio. Use a glass jar with a tight-fitting lid.

2. Put the jar in a cool, dark location for two weeks.

3. Shake the jar every day for a minute.

4. Strain the solids out of the alcohol, reserving both separately. Squeeze all the liquid out of the mushroom chunks.

5. Make a 1:20 ratio with the solids and the 95% alcohol.

6. Simmer the 1:20 mixture until it is reduced by half.
7. Cool and strain the mixture.
8. Combine the strained mixture with the reserved decoction.

Dual Extraction (also referred to as Double Extraction)

This method combines water extraction with alcohol extraction to receive the benefits of both. Chaga and Reishi, in particular, benefit from this method. It is best to do the water extraction first, followed by alcohol extraction.
This is not ideal for all mushrooms though. There are some mushrooms that, if an alcohol extraction is used, the important active ingredients will deteriorate or be filtered out entirely.

<u>Best mushrooms for Dual Extraction</u>: Chaga, Reishi, Turkey Tail.

1. In a quart-sized glass jar, add dried mushrooms to fill it up halfway.

2. Fill the rest of the jar with 80-proof or higher alcohol, leaving a 1-inch gap at the top.
3. Tightly affix lid.

4. Place in a cool, dry location for 30 days. *Shake every day for 1 minute.*

5. Strain the solids from the alcohol, reserving both.
6. Take the solid mushroom pieces that were strained and add them to a pot. Cover with 2 quarts cold water and bring to a simmer (do not boil!).

7. Simmer 1-2 hours or until water is reduced by half.

8. Turn off heat and let it cool.
9. Strain out solid pieces, reserving the liquid.

10 Combine the liquid from the alcohol extraction with the liquid from the water extraction.

11. Store in a cool, dark location for best storage.

Cooking Fresh Mushrooms

All fresh mushrooms should be cooked before eating. Raw mushrooms may make you ill. All wild mushrooms must be cooked before consumption as they can contain dangerous levels of agaritine and other toxins.

Mushrooms that can be cooked & eaten:
*mushrooms in italics are choice edibles
- Horse Mushroom
- Button Mushroom/Portobello/Crimini
- Field Mushroom

- Almond Mushroom
- Jelly Ear Fungus
- *Enoki*
- *Maitake*
- *Lion's Mane/Hericium sp.*
- *Chicken of the Woods (all types)*
- *Shiitake*
- Cordyceps
- Oyster mushroom (all types)

Matsutake

A recent study showed that grilling or microwaving mushrooms is the best way to cook them as these methods retain the most nutrients.[316] Frying, sautéing, and boiling are all fine methods, as well, but many nutrients and proteins are lost in the process.

Preparing mushrooms to eat and also retaining their medicinal properties is a fine balance. Mushrooms should be cooked for a minimum of 5-10 minutes to remove the properties that cause gastrointestinal upset.

All the mushrooms in the above list, except for Jelly Ear Fungus, can be added to any dish: stir-fries, salads, used as a meat substitute, added to pasta, soups, stews, or served on their own.

Jelly Ear Fungus has a rubbery-type consistency and many consider it an acquired taste. It's not a mushroom that most people will enjoy eating on its own. It works best in a soup or stew, chopped finely so as not to be noticeable.

Grilling or Broiling Mushrooms

The time needed to grill depends on the size and type of mushroom. They can be cleaned and grilled or marinated first, then grilled. Grilling and broiling are done the same way.

1. Clean mushrooms gently with water. Pat dry.
2. Marinate, if desired, for 2-4 hours.
3. Heat grill.
4. If mushrooms aren't marinated, brush each one lightly with oil.
5. Grill 4-6 minutes on each side.
6. Brush with more oil or marinade as they are cooking, as needed.
7. Test for tenderness, some may take longer.
8. Serve.

Microwaving Mushrooms

The exact time depends on the size and type of mushroom.

1. Slice mushrooms thickly.
2. Place in a microwave-safe bowl.
3. There is no need to add oil or water. Mushrooms contain a lot of water naturally and will release lots during the cooking process.
4. Cover loosely.
5. Microwave 2-3 minutes, or until tender.
6. Eat plain or use as a component in another dish.

Roasting Mushrooms

1. Preheat the oven to 450F (230C).
2. Place cleaned mushrooms in a bowl.
3. Lightly toss with olive oil or high-temperature oil of choice.
4. Spread mushrooms out in a single layer on a baking sheet.
5. Roast for 20 minutes, checking and turning them after 10 minutes.
6. After 20 minutes, check for tenderness. Roast longer, if necessary.

Sautéing Mushrooms

Most mushrooms have a high water content, though it varies greatly between types. The maturity of mushrooms also makes a difference. Young Chicken of the Woods is high in moisture while older specimens can be quite dry.

1. Heat a sauté pan to medium-high.
2. Add cleaned mushrooms.
3. Dry sauté the mushrooms until they release all their moisture.
4. As the mushrooms release moisture, drain it off (carefully!) in the sink. It may take several times to get all the moisture out. Be patient.
5. When the mushrooms are relatively dry and start sticking to the pan, turn down the heat to medium.
6. Add butter or oil, salt, and any other seasonings, and sauté until golden brown.

Cooking With Polypores

Polypores can be used in cooking and then removed before being served. They are best used in soups and broths that require simmering for a length of time. Polypores are tough, often woody, and can have quite strong flavors.

Polypore Mushrooms

- Turkey Tail
- Birch Polypore
- Agarikon
- Red-Banded Polypore
- Reishi
- Chaga
- Black Hoof Mushroom
- Stout Camphor Fungus

Polypore Mushroom Basic Preparation (from fresh)

1. Cut up the polypore into medium chunks (so you can find them later when removing them).
2. Add 30 grams (1 ounce) to soup or broth.
3. Simmer for a minimum of 30 minutes.
4. Remove chunks before consuming.[317]

Polypore Mushroom Basic Preparation (from dried)

1. Soak dried mushroom pieces in water for a minimum of 8 hours.
2. Strain and reserve mushroom water.
3. Simmer mushroom water 5-10 minutes.

4. Add to soup or broth, or drink as a tea.

Polypore Mushroom Tea

1. Cut thin slices of the polypore mushroom and place it in a pan with water.
2. Simmer for a minimum of 30 minutes to extract active properties.
3. Other herbs or tea can be added to help with the taste.
4. Remove mushroom pieces before drinking.

Chaga Tea Preparation

The preparation for Chaga varies from other polypores because it cannot be sliced. It is extremely hard and needs to be broken up into chunks with a hammer or the like. Small pieces can be ground into a powder in a strong food processor. Chaga has a surprisingly sweet taste; it isn't unpleasant consumed on its own but it may not be to everyone's taste preference. Combining with another tea or adding it to coffee are popular options.

Hajai Photo/Shutterstock.com

Chaga Tea Basic Recipe

1. Break up 2-4 ounces Chaga into 1" or smaller pieces.
2. Combine in a pot with 4 cups (1 liter) water.
3. Bring to a simmer and slow simmer for two hours. [do not let it boil, boiling kills antioxidants.]
4. Remove from heat and let cool.
5. Strain out chunks. [They can be saved and reused for another batch if desired.]
6. Store Chaga tea in a glass bottle in the refrigerator for 2-3 months.
7. To serve, pour into a cup with a little of your favorite sweetener.

Reishi Tea Preparation

A bitter-tasting mushroom, Reishi is best combined with other strong flavors and some sweetener.

ladymove_joon/Shutterstock.com

Reishi Tea Basic Recipe

1. Add 6-8 pieces of sliced Reishi (fresh or dried) to 4 cups (1 liter) water in a saucepan.
2. Bring to simmer and simmer 20 minutes [do not boil].
3. Remove from heat.
4. Add crushed mint leaves and sweetener to taste.
5. Let steep 30 minutes.
6. Strain out Reishi pieces.
7. Serve as is.
8. Store leftover in refrigerator up to 7-14 days.

Other good additions to help with taste and improve medicinal properties: fresh or dried ginger, chamomile, green tea.

Cosmetic Applications

Birch Polypore Oil for Skin

1. Thinly slice polypore and place it in a crockpot.
2. Add monounsaturated vegetable oil in a 1:5 ratio.
3. Set it on low for six hours.
4. Remove from crockpot and strain out solid material (cheesecloth works well here).
5. Store in a glass jar.
6. Use as a skin conditioner.

Mushroom Preparation by Type

Some mushrooms are easy to find fresh or dried. Others are more difficult. At the end of this section, I have compiled a list of sources.

MUSHROOM	EAT FRESH (Y/N)	OPTIONS	CAUTIONS
Agaricus arvensis (Horse Mushroom)	Yes	Fresh, supplements	
Agaricus bisporus (Button, Crimini, Portobello)	Yes	Fresh, powder, supplement	
Agaricus campestris (Field Mushroom)	Yes	Fresh	

Agaricus subrufescens (Almond Mushroom)	Yes	Fresh, supplement	
Auricularia auricula-judae (Jelly Ear Fungus)	Yes	Fresh, dried, extract	May interfere with anticoagulants. May interfere with fertility – do not take if pregnant, nursing, or while trying to conceive.
Coriolus versicolor	No	Tea, tincture, capsule, powder, extract	May cause dark stools
Flammulina velutipes (Enoki)	Yes	Fresh, dried, tincture, capsule	Contains cardiotoxic which is eradicated with heating. Do not eat raw.
Fomitopsis betulina (Birch Polypore)	No	Dried, tincture	
Fomitopsis officinalis (Agarikon)	No	Dried, tincture, powder, extract	
Fomitopsis pincola (Red-Banded Polypore)	No	Dried, extract	
Ganoderma lucidum (Reishi)	No	Dried, capsules, tincture, tea, powder, extracts	May interfere with anticoagulants
Grifola frondosa (Maitake)	Yes	Fresh, dried, powder, extract, tincture,	

		capsules	
Hericium sp. (Lion's Mane and other Hericium types)	Yes	Fresh, dried, capsules, pills, tinctures, powders, tea	
Hydnellum peckii (Devil's Tooth)	No	Not available	
Inonotuus obliquus (Chaga)	No	Dried, capsules, tinctures, pills, tea, powder, extracts	May interfere with anticoagulants and insulin. Potential strain on the kidneys. Chaga grows on birch trees; if you have a birch allergy, do not use this.
Laetiporus sulphureus (Chicken of the Woods)	Yes	Fresh, dried	
Lentinula edodes (Shiitake)	Yes	Fresh, dried, capsules, pills, extracts, capsules	Purine content may cause gout flare-ups
Lignosus rhinocerus (Tiger's Milk)	No	Capsule, powder	
Ophiocordyceps sinensis (Cordyceps)	Yes	Fresh, dried, capsules, powders, tinctures, extracts, tea	May interfere with anticoagulants and diabetes medications. People with autoimmune disorders shouldn't take this – if unsure, consult a doctor beforehand. May

			interfere with hormone imbalance medications.
Panellus stipticus (Bitter Oyster)	No	Dried	
Phellinus linteus (Black Hoof)	No	Powder, capsules	
Pleurotus ostreatus (Oyster Mushroom [all Pleurotus sp.]	Yes	Fresh, dried, powder, capsules	May interfere with protease inhibitors
Taiwanofungus camphoratus (Stout Camphor)	No	Extract, tincture, tea, capsule	May interfere with anticoagulants
Tolypocladium inflatum	No	Not available	
Tricholoma Matsutake (Matsutak)	Yes	Fresh, dried	

Recommended Dosages by Mushroom

The exact amount a person needs to receive medicinal benefits will vary based on age, weight, and current health. These factors are best assessed and determined by a doctor. There is no one-size-fits-all formula. In this text, we suggest doses but it should not replace advice from a medical professional.

Additionally, as with all foods, it is entirely possible some types of mushrooms may cause an allergic reaction or gastrointestinal upset. If you've never had a specific mushroom, try small amounts first. This does not mean the mushrooms are dangerous to consume. All foods are potential allergens: peanuts, garlic, soy, and gluten are a few of the more common ones affecting people today. Mushrooms are no different. Each one in the list of medicinals is different; having an unpleasant reaction with one does not indicate how you will react to another.

Guidelines for taking new medicinals:

1. Take ¼ of the recommended dose, to start, in case of adverse reactions.
2. Increase the dosage slowly, until at 2 weeks the recommended dose is reached.
3. More isn't always better. Pay attention to dosages; they are there for a reason.
4. If you have a compromised immune system, are taking prescription medicines, are pregnant, or trying to get pregnant, always consult a doctor before taking new medicines.

All amounts are recommendations.

Agaricus arvensis (Horse Mushroom)

Eaten fresh, 4-8oz.

Agaricus bisporus (Button, Crimini, Portobello)

Eaten fresh, 4-8oz.

Agaricus campestris (Field Mushroom)

Eaten fresh, 4-8oz.

Agaricus subrufescens (Almond Mushroom)

Eaten fresh, 4-8oz.

For cancer, 3 grams per day.[318]

Auricularia auricula-judae (Jelly Ear Fungus)

Eaten fresh, 1-2 oz.
General-use, 2-3 grams extract per day.

Coriolus versicolor

General use, 2-3 grams extract per day.

For cancer, 3-6 grams extract per day.
For immune support, 1-2 grams extract per day.

Flammulina velutipes (Enoki)

Dried, 8-9 grams per day.[319]
Fresh, 30-50 grams per day.

For neurodegenerative issues, 3-5 grams per day.[320]

Fomitopsis betulina (Birch Polypore)

General use, 1 teaspoon tincture twice a day.
Tea, 2-3 8oz cups per day (3-12 grams dried mushroom).

Fomitopsis officinalis (Agarikon)

General use, 10-20 grams per day.

Fomitopsis pincola (Red-Banded Polypore)

General use, 20-30 grams twice daily.

Ganoderma lucidum (Reishi)

Tea, 100-200ml/day (3/4 cup).
Tincture, 2-3 droppers per day (2-3ml total)[321] or for targeted use, 10ml 3x/day.[322]
Dried or Fresh, 3-5 grams/day.

For allergies, 500mg extract 3x/day.
For asthma, 1-3 grams extract per day.
For cancer, 2-5 grams extract per day.
For cardiovascular health, 1-3 grams extract per day.[323]
For insomnia, 1-3 grams extract per day.
For rheumatoid arthritis, 1-3 grams extract per day.[324]

Grifola frondosa (Maitake)

Fresh, 3-7 grams/day or more.[325]
D or MD-Fraction specialty extracts, 35-150mg per day.

For PCOS (polycystic ovary syndrome), 3 grams per day.[326]

Hericium sp. (Lion's Mane and other Hericium types)

Tea, 100ml 2-3 times per day (1/3 cup).[327]
Dried, 3-5 grams per day.

For Alzheimer's, 3-5 grams/day.
For depression, 3-5 grams/day.
For gastric ulcer, 25-50 grams day (fruiting body).
For MRSA, 25 grams per day (fruiting body).
For nerve damage, 3-5 grams per day.[328]

Hydnellum peckii (Devil's Tooth) – not available commercially

Inonotuus obliquus (Chaga)

Dried, 1/2 teaspoon per day (2.5oz).
Tincture, 2-3 droppers per day (2-3ml total).
Tea, 1-2 6oz cups per day.[329]

For cancer, 2-5 grams extract per day.
For psoriasis, 2-3 grams extract per day.[330]

Laetiporus sulphureus (Chicken of the Woods)

Fresh, 4-6 oz. per day.

Lentinula edodes (Shiitake)

Fresh, 3-5 oz. /day.
Dried, 2-6 grams/day.[331]

For immune support, 2-6 grams extract per day.
For high cholesterol, 9-15 grams per day (fruiting body).[332]

Lignosus rhinocerus (Tiger's Milk)

General use, 250-500 mg/day.

Ophiocordyceps sinensis (Cordyceps)

Tea, 100ml (1/3 cup) per day.
General use, 2-3 grams per day.

For cancer, 2-5 grams extract per day.
For diabetes, 3-5 grams per day.
For libido, 3 grams per day.
For kidney function, 3 grams per day.[333]

Panellus stipticus (Bitter Oyster)

Used to stop bleeding, apply fresh or dried.

Phellinus linteus (Black Hoof)

Dried, 10-30 grams per day.
General use, 2-3 grams extract per day.

For rheumatoid arthritis, 3 grams extract per day.[334]

Pleurotus ostreatus (Oyster Mushroom) & all Pleurotus sp.

Dried, 3-9 grams/day.[335]
Fresh, 2-3 grams per day.

General use, 1-2 grams extract per day.

For high cholesterol, 15-20 grams per day (dried).[336]

Taiwanofungus camphoratus (Stout Camphor)

1-3 grams/day.

For liver disease and cancer, 1-3 grams extract per day.[337]

Tolypocladium inflatum – not available commercially.

Tricholoma Matsutake (Matsutake)

Fresh or dried, 4-8 oz. /per day.

Resources for Intake Recommendations:

Powell, Martin. *Medicinal Mushrooms: the Essential Guide.* Mycology Press, 2013.
Hobbs, Christopher. *Medicinal Mushrooms: an Exploration of Tradition, Healing, & Culture.* Botanica Press, 2003.
Zhao, Yanyi, et al. *Pharmacopoeia of the Peoples Republic of China 2015.* China Medical Science Press, 2015.
Fungicopia, Medicinal Mushrooms. *Fungicopia*
https://www.fungicopia.com/medicinalmushrooms

CHAPTER 8

SOURCING MUSHROOMS

Foraging

Do not collect mushroom species on your own unless you are experienced or are with an experienced forager. Many of the mushrooms listed here have look-a-likes that will make you ill. Mushroom foraging takes time, practice, and dedication.

To source fresh mushrooms, look for a local forager in your area and check their references. There are many hobbyists, and all consumption of fresh mushrooms is at your own risk. That all being said, mushroom foraging is a lot of fun and an excellent skill to learn. There are mycology groups across the world who are open to teaching newcomers the basics of foraging.

Jaime Montemayor/Shutterstock.com

Buying Fresh

Mushrooms like Agaricus bisporus (button mushrooms) and Pleurotus ostreatus (oyster mushrooms) are widely available around the world. Sadly, those are the only ones that can be found with regularity. Shiitake and Enoki can also be found easily in parts of the world. However, for many, they are quite difficult to find fresh. The availability of mushrooms greatly depends on where you live and the culture around eating mushrooms. For example, in the United States, eating mushrooms other than Agaricus bisporus, is not widely practiced. In China and most other Asian countries, eating mushrooms of all varieties is standard and time-honored. With the advent of online shopping and increased access to resources, some types of mushrooms can now be ordered via the web. It is important to choose a supplier with a good reputation since the misclassification of mushrooms or unsafe growing methods can greatly impact what you receive.

Buying Dried, Capsules, Tinctures, Preparations

As with all methods, research the supplier well before buying. All mushrooms can be dried for resale. A traditional medicine practitioner may have a brand they recommend or one they make themselves. In this text, the difference between extracts, tinctures, and double-extractions is discussed. Please use this information when preparing to purchase any supplements – they type you get may make a difference.

Marilyn Barbone/Shutterstock.com

Supplement Sources in the United States

The dosages of supplements vary, and people should follow the instructions on the label carefully. It is also advisable to discuss the use of any new supplement with a doctor.

Mushroom Science - Extracts & Supplements
FreshCap – Extracts, Powders, Supplements
Host Defense – Extracts, Powders, Supplements, Sprays

Conclusion

Mushrooms are extremely varied in type and efficacy in treating health conditions and concerns. The field of medicinal mushrooms is still new in the western world, though there are hundreds of years of use in Asia and Europe. Studies are being conducted frequently using scientific methods to determine the exact medicinal components. Mushrooms offer an opportunity to treat disease with natural methods without the side effects of most western medicines. The most-studied fungi, like Chaga, Reishi, Cordyceps, and Lion's Mane, are proven to have medicinal properties. From the time penicillin was discovered in 1928, mushrooms have continued to impress the medical world with their power and effectiveness. The fungi kingdom is broad and there is still much to come as we open our eyes and continue the study of their medicinal values.

ABOUT THE AUTHOR

Richard's father was a keen gardener and that is where his interest in all natural things began. As a youngster, he enjoyed nothing better than helping his father in the garden.

Nowadays, he finds himself at the opposite end of life. Having had a satisfying career, he now has time to potter around in his garden and take care of his small homestead. Much of the food on his dinner table is homegrown. He likes to experiment with various gardening methods and find new ways to grow bountiful crops year-round.

He wants to share his knowledge and show how easy and rewarding it is to set up your own prosperous garden and apply the healing power of plants. In his opinion, you don't need a huge budget to get started. When you do get started, you will soon feel, and taste, the benefits of growing your own healthy and healing food.

Learn more about Richard Bray at
amazon.com/author/richardbray

1 World Health Organization, Cancer Facts, 12 Sept, 2018.

2 Dresch P, D Aguanno MN, Rosam K, Grienke U, Rollinger JM, Peintner U. Fungal strain matters: colony growth and bioactivity of the European medicinal polypores Fomes fomentarius, Fomitopsis pinicola and Piptoporus betulinus. AMB Express. 2015;5(1):4. Published 2015 Jan 24. doi:10.1186/s13568-014-0093-0

3 Matsui, Yoichi et al.,Improved prognosis of postoperative hepatocellular carcinoma patients when treated with functional foods: a prospective cohort study, Journal of Hepatology, Volume 37, Issue 1, 78 - 86

4 Nakazato H, Koike A, Saji S, Ogawa N, Sakamoto J. Efficacy of immunochemotherapy as adjuvant treatment after curative resection of gastric cancer. Study Group of Immunochemotherapy with PSK for Gastric Cancer. Lancet. 1994 May 7;343(8906):1122-6. PubMed PMID: 7910230.

5 Hirahara N, Edamatsu T, Fujieda A, Fujioka M, Wada T, Tajima Y. Protein-bound polysaccharide-K (PSK) induces apoptosis via p38 mitogen-activated protein kinase pathway in promyelomonocytic leukemia HL-60 cells. Anticancer Res. 2012 Jul;32(7):2631-7. PubMed PMID: 22753720.

6 Ohwada S, Ikeya T, Yokomori T, Kusaba T, Roppongi T, Takahashi T, Nakamura S, Kakinuma S, Iwazaki S, Ishikawa H, Kawate S, Nakajima T, Morishita Y. Adjuvant immunochemotherapy with oral Tegafur/Uracil plus PSK in patients with stage II or III colorectal cancer: a randomised controlled study. Br J Cancer. 2004 Mar 8;90(5):1003-10.

7 Torisu M, Hayashi Y, Ishimitsu T, Fujimura T, Iwasaki K, Katano M, Yamamoto H, Kimura Y, Takesue M, Kondo M, et al. Significant prolongation of disease-free period gained by oral polysaccharide K (PSK) administration after curative surgical operation of colorectal cancer. Cancer Immunol Immunother. 1990;31(5):261-8. PubMed PMID: 2198088.

8 Tsang KW, Lam CL, Yan C, Mak JC, Ooi GC, Ho JC, Lam B, Man R, Sham JS, Lam WK. Coriolus versicolor polysaccharide peptide slows progression of advanced non-small cell lung cancer. Respir Med. 2003 Jun;97(6):618-24. PubMed PMID: 12814145.

9 Dogan A, Dalar A, Sadullahoglu C, Battal A, Uzun Y, Celik I, Demirel K. Investigation of the protective effects of horse mushroom (Agaricus arvensis Schaeff.) against carbon tetrachloride-induced oxidative stress in rats. Mol Biol Rep. 2018 Oct;45(5):787-797

10 Çavuşlar Atila, Funda & Owaid, Mustafa & Shariati, Mohammad Ali. (2017). The nutritional and medical benefits of Agaricus Bisporus: A review. Journal of microbiology, biotechnology and food sciences. 7. 10.15414/jmbfs.2017/18.7.3.281-286.

11 Kosanić, Marijana & Ranković, Branislav & Stanojkovic, Tatjana. (2017). BIOACTIVITY OF EDIBLE MUSHROOM AGARICUS CAMPESTRIS.

12 Kim YW, Kim KH, Choi HJ, Lee DS. Anti-diabetic activity of beta-glucans and their enzymatically hydrolyzed oligosaccharides from Agaricus blazei. Biotechnol Lett. 2005 Apr;27(7):483-7. PubMed PMID: 15928854.

13 Liu Y, Fukuwatari Y, Okumura K, Takeda K, Ishibashi K, Furukawa M, Ohno N, Mori K, Gao M, Motoi M. Immunomodulating Activity of Agaricus brasiliensis KA21 in Mice and in Human Volunteers. Evid Based Complement Alternat Med. 2008 Jun;5(2):205-19. doi: 10.1093/ecam/nem016. PubMed PMID: 18604247;

14 Therkelsen SP, Hetland G, Lyberg T, Lygren I, Johnson E. Effect of a Medicinal Agaricus blazei Murill-Based Mushroom Extract, AndoSan™, on Symptoms, Fatigue and Quality of Life in Patients with Ulcerative Colitis in a Randomized Single-Blinded Placebo Controlled Study. PLoS One. 2016 Mar 2;11(3):e0150191.doi: 10.1371/journal.pone.0150191.

15 Ahn WS, Kim DJ, Chae GT, Lee JM, Bae SM, Sin JI, Kim YW, Namkoong SE, Lee IP. Natural killer cell activity and quality of life were improved by consumption of a mushroom extract, Agaricus blazei Murill Kyowa, in gynecological cancer patients undergoing chemotherapy. Int J Gynecol Cancer. 2004 Jul-Aug;14(4):589-94

16 Val, C.H., Brant, F., Miranda, A.S. et al. Effect of mushroom Agaricus blazei on immune response and development of experimental cerebral malaria. Malar J 14, 311 (2015).

17 Sękara, Agnieszka & Kalisz, Andrzej & Grabowska, Aneta & Siwulski, Marek. (2015). Auricularia spp. - mushrooms as Novel Food and therapeutic agents - a review. Sydowia -Horn-. 67. 1-10. 10.12905/0380.sydowia67-2015-0001.

18 Yuan, Z et al. "Hypoglycemic effect of water-soluble polysaccharide from Auricularia auricula-judae Quel. on genetically diabetic KK-Ay mice." Bioscience, biotechnology, and biochemistry 62 10 (1998): 1898-903 .

19 Elkhateeb, Waill & Daba, Ghoson & Elnahas, Marwa & Thomas, Paul. (2019). Anticoagulant Capacities of Some Medicinal Mushrooms. Journal of Pharmaceutical Sciences. 5. 12-16.

20 Sękara, Agnieszka & Kalisz, Andrzej & Grabowska, Aneta & Siwulski, Marek. (2015). Auricularia spp. - mushrooms as Novel Food and therapeutic agents - a review. Sydowia -Horn-. 67. 1-10. 10.12905/0380.sydowia67-2015-0001.

21 Zhuan-Yun LI, Xue-Ping Y, Bin L, et al. Auricularia auricular-judae polysaccharide attenuates lipopolysaccharide-induced acute lung injury by inhibiting oxidative stress and inflammation. Biomed Rep. 2015;3(4):478–482. doi:10.3892/br.2015.470

22 Packialakshmi B, Sudha G and Charumathy M: Studies on phytochemical compounds and antioxidant potential of *Auricularia auricula-judae*. Int J Pharm Sci Res 2017; 8(8): 3508-15.doi: 10.13040/IJPSR.0975-8232.8(8).3508-15.

23 Niimoto M, Hattori T, Tamada R, Sugimachi K, Inokuchi K, Ogawa N. Postoperative adjuvant immunochemotherapy with mitomycin C, futraful and PSK for gastric cancer. An analysis of data on 579 patients followed for five years. Jpn J Surg. 1988 Nov;18(6):681-6.

24 Toth B, Coles M, Lynch J. Effects of VPS extract of Coriolus versicolor on cancer of the large intestine using a serial sacrifice technique. In Vivo. 2006 May-Jun;20(3):341-6.

25 Iino Y, Yokoe T, Maemura M, Horiguchi J, Takei H, Ohwada S, Morishita Y. Immunochemotherapies versus chemotherapy as adjuvant treatment after curative resection of operable breast cancer. Anticancer Res. 1995 Nov-Dec;15(6B):2907-11.

26 Tsang KW, Lam CL, Yan C, Mak JC, Ooi GC, Ho JC, Lam B, Man R, Sham JS, Lam WK. Coriolus versicolor polysaccharide peptide slows progression of advanced non-small cell lung cancer. Respir Med. 2003 Jun;97(6):618-24.

27 Jiang J, Sliva D. Novel medicinal mushroom blend suppresses growth and invasiveness of human breast cancer cells. Int J Oncol. 2010 Dec;37(6):1529-36.

28 Xian HM, Che H, Qin Y, Yang F, Meng SY, Li XG, Bai YL, Wang LH. Coriolus versicolor aqueous extract ameliorates insulin resistance with PI3K/Akt and p38 MAPK signaling pathways involved in diabetic skeletal muscle. Phytother Res. 2018 Mar;32(3):551-560. doi: 10.1002/ptr.6007.

29 Tang C, Hoo PC, Tan LT, et al. Golden Needle Mushroom: A Culinary Medicine with Evidenced-Based Biological Activities and Health Promoting Properties. *Front Pharmacol.* 2016;7:474. Published 2016 Dec 7. doi:10.3389/fphar.2016.00474

30 Capasso, Luigi, 5300 years ago, the Ice Man used natural laxatives and antibiotics. The Lancet, Dec 05, 1998. Vol 352, P1864.

31 Pleszczyńska M, Wiater A, Siwulski M, et al. Cultivation and utility of Piptoporus betulinus fruiting bodies as a source of anticancer agents. *World J Microbiol Biotechnol.* 2016;32(9):151. doi:10.1007/s11274-016-2114-4

32 Ulrike Grienke, Margit Zöll, Ursula Peintner, Judith M. Rollinger, European medicinal polypores – A modern view on traditional uses, Journal of Ethnopharmacology, Volume 154, Issue 3, 2014, Pages 564-583, ISSN 0378-8741

33 Kyung Mo Kim, Yuh-Gang Yoon & Hack Sung Jung (2005) Evaluation of the monophyly of *Fomitopsis* using parsimony and MCMC methods, Mycologia, 97:4, 812-822, DOI: 10.1080/15572536.2006.11832773

34 Cornell University, Cornell University Blog, Agarikon, Apr 10, 2010, https://blog.mycology.cornell.edu/2010/04/12/agarikon/

35 Girometta C. Antimicrobial properties of Fomitopsis officinalis in the light of its bioactive metabolites: a review. Mycology. 2018 Oct 25;10(1):32-39. doi:10.1080/21501203.2018.1536680. eCollection 2019 Mar. Review.

36 Ulrike Grienke, Margit Zöll, Ursula Peintner, Judith M. Rollinger, European medicinal polypores – A modern view on traditional uses, Journal of Ethnopharmacology, Volume 154, Issue 3, 2014, Pages 564-583, ISSN 0378-8741

37 Cornell University, Cornell University Blog, Ganoderma lucidum and G. Tsugae, Oct 30, 2006. https://blog.mycology.cornell.edu/2006/10/30/introducing-ganoderma-lucidum-and-g-tsugae/comment-page-1/

38 Jin X, Ruiz Beguerie J, Sze DM, Chan GC. Ganoderma lucidum (Reishi mushroom) for cancer treatment. Cochrane Database Syst Rev. 2012 Jun 13;(6):CD007731. doi: 10.1002/14651858.CD007731.pub2. Review. Update in: Cochrane Database Syst Rev. 2016;4:CD007731.

39 Bao YX, Wong CK, Li EK, Tam LS, Leung PC, Yin YB, Lam CW. Immunomodulatory effects of lingzhi and san-miao-san supplementation on patients with rheumatoid arthritis. Immunopharmacol Immunotoxicol. 2006;28(2):197-200.

40 Kim KC, Jun HJ, Kim JS, Kim IG. Enhancement of radiation response with combined Ganoderma lucidum and Duchesnea chrysantha extracts in human leukemia HL-60 cells. Int J Mol Med. 2008 Apr;21(4):489-98.

41 Roldan-Deamicis A, Alonso E, Brie B, Braico DA, Balogh GA. Maitake Pro4X has anti-cancer activity and prevents oncogenesis in BALBc mice. Cancer Med. 2016 Sep;5(9):2427-41. doi: 10.1002/cam4.744. Epub 2016 Jul 11.

42 Zhang Y, Sun D, Meng Q, Guo W, Chen Q, Zhang Y. Grifola frondosa polysaccharides induce breast cancer cell apoptosis via the mitochondrial-dependent apoptotic pathway. Int J Mol Med. 2017 Oct;40(4):1089-1095. doi: 10.3892/ijmm.2017.3081.

43 Fang J, Wang Y, Lv X, Shen X, Ni X, Ding K. Structure of a β-glucan from Grifola frondosa and its antitumor effect by activating Dectin-1/Syk/NF-κB signaling. Glycoconj J. 2012 Aug;29(5-6):365-77.

44 Hong L, Xun M, Wutong W. Anti-diabetic effect of an alpha-glucan from fruit body of maitake (Grifola frondosa) on KK-Ay mice. J Pharm Pharmacol. 2007 Apr;59(4):575-82.

205

45 Masuda Y, Murata Y, Hayashi M, Nanba H. Inhibitory effect of MD-Fraction on tumor metastasis: involvement of NK cell activation and suppression of intercellular adhesion molecule (ICAM)-1 expression in lung vascular endothelial cells. Biol Pharm Bull. 2008 Jun;31(6):1104-8.

46 Spelman, Kevin & Sutherland, Elizabeth & Bagade, Aravind. (2017). Neurological Activity of Lion's Mane (Hericium erinaceus). Journal of Restorative Medicine. 6. 19-26. 10.14200/jrm.2017.6.0108.

47 Khan, Md. Asaduzzaman & Tania, Mousumi & Liu, Rui & Rahman, Mohammad Mijanur. (2013). Hericium erinaceus: An edible mushroom with medicinal values. Journal of complementary & integrative medicine. 10. 1-6. 10.1515/jcim-2013-0001.

48 Elkhateeb, Waill & Daba, Ghoson & Elnahas, Marwa & Thomas, Paul. (2019). Anticoagulant Capacities of Some Medicinal Mushrooms. Journal of Pharmaceutical Sciences. 5. 12-16.

49 Zhong XH, Ren K, Lu SJ, Yang SY, Sun DZ. Progress of research on Inonotus obliquus. Chin J Integr Med. 2009 Apr;15(2):156-60. doi: 10.1007/s11655-009-0156-2. Epub 2009 Apr 29.

50 Glamočlija J, Ćirić A, Nikolić M, Fernandes Â, Barros L, Calhelha RC, Ferreira IC, Soković M, van Griensven LJ. Chemical characterization and biological activity of Chaga (Inonotus obliquus), a medicinal "mushroom". J Ethnopharmacol. 2015 Mar 13;162:323-32. doi: 10.1016/j.jep.2014.12.069. Epub 2015 Jan 7.

51 Khatua S, Ghosh S, Acharya K. Laetiporus sulphureus (Bull.: Fr.) Murr. as Food as Medicine. Pharmacog J. 2017;9(6s):s1-s15.

52 Yang H, Hwang I, Kim S, Hong EJ, Jeung EB. Lentinus edodes promotes fat removal in hypercholesterolemic mice. Exp Ther Med. 2013 Dec;6(6):1409-1413. Epub 2013 Oct 8.

53 Ngai PH, Ng TB. Lentin, a novel and potent antifungal protein from shitake mushroom with inhibitory effects on activity of human immunodeficiency virus-1 reverse transcriptase and proliferation of leukemia cells. Life Sci. 2003 Nov 14;73(26):3363-74.

54 Dai X, Stanilka JM, Rowe CA, Esteves EA, Nieves C Jr, Spaiser SJ, Christman MC, Langkamp-Henken B, Percival SS. Consuming Lentinula edodes (Shiitake) Mushrooms Daily Improves Human Immunity: A Randomized Dietary Intervention in Healthy Young Adults. J Am Coll Nutr. 2015;34(6):478-87. doi: 10.1080/07315724.2014.950391. Epub 2015 Apr 11.

55 Wang KP, Zhang QL, Liu Y, Wang J, Cheng Y, Zhang Y. Structure and inducing tumor cell apoptosis activity of polysaccharides isolated from Lentinus edodes. J Agric Food Chem. 2013 Oct 16;61(41):9849-58. doi: 10.1021/jf403291w.

56 Lee, Sookshien & Tan, Nget & Fung, Shin & Sim, Si Mui & Tan, Chon-Seng & Ng, Szu. (2014). Anti-inflammatory effect of the sclerotium of Lignosus rhinocerotis (Cooke) Ryvarden, the Tiger Milk mushroom. BMC complementary and alternative medicine. 14. 359. 10.1186/1472-6882-14-359.

57 Nallathamby N, Serm LG, Raman J, Malek SNA, Vidyadaran S, Naidu M, Kuppusamy UR, Sabaratnama V. Identification and in vitro Evaluation of Lipids from Sclerotia of Lignosus rhinocerotis for Antioxidant and Anti-neuroinflammatory Activities. Nat Prod Commun. 2016 Oct;11(10):1485-1490.

58 Hong T, Zhang M, Fan J. Cordyceps sinensis (a traditional Chinese medicine) for kidney transplant recipients. Cochrane Database Syst Rev. 2015 Oct 12;(10):CD009698. doi: 10.1002/14651858.CD009698.pub2.

59 Zhu JS, Halpern GM, Jones K. The scientific rediscovery of an ancient Chinese herbal medicine: Cordyceps sinensis: part I. J Altern Complement Med. 1998 Fall;4(3):289-303.

60 Zhu JS, Halpern GM, Jones K. The scientific rediscovery of a precious ancient Chinese herbal regimen: Cordyceps sinensis: part II. J Altern Complement Med. 1998 Winter;4(4):429-57.

61 Zhu T, Kim SH, Chen CY. A medicinal mushroom: Phellinus linteus. Curr Med Chem. 2008;15(13):1330-5.

62 Konno S, Chu K, Feuer N, Phillips J, Choudhury M. Potent Anticancer Effects of Bioactive Mushroom Extracts (Phellinus linteus) on a Variety of Human Cancer Cells. J Clin Med Res. 2015 Feb;7(2):76-82. doi: 10.14740/jocmr1996w. Epub 2014 Nov 19.

63 Sliva D. Medicinal mushroom Phellinus linteus as an alternative cancer therapy. Exp Ther Med. 2010;1(3):407–411. doi:10.3892/etm_00000063

64 Chandimali N, Huynh DL, Jin WY, Kwon T. Combination Effects of Hispidin and Gemcitabine via Inhibition of Stemness in Pancreatic Cancer Stem Cells. Anticancer Res. 2018 Jul;38(7):3967-3975. doi: 10.21873/anticanres.12683.

65 Chen W, Tan H, Liu Q, et al. A Review: The Bioactivities and Pharmacological Applications of Phellinus linteus. Molecules. 2019;24(10):1888. Published 2019 May 16. doi:10.3390/molecules24101888

66 Su H -H, Chu Y -C, Liao J -M, Wang Y -H, Jan M -S, Lin C-W, Wu C-Y, Tseng C-Y, Yen J -C and Huang S-S (2017) Phellinus linteus Mycelium Alleviates Myocardial Ischemia-Reperfusion Injury through Autophagic Regulation. Front. Pharmacol. 8:175. doi: 10.3389/fphar.2017.00175

67 Hagiwara SY, Takahashi M, Shen Y, Kaihou S, Tomiyama T, Yazawa M, Tamai Y, SinY, Kazusaka A, Terazawa M. A phytochemical in the edible Tamogi-take mushroom (Pleurotus cornucopiae), D-mannitol, inhibits ACE activity and lowers the blood pressure of spontaneously hypertensive rats. Biosci Biotechnol Biochem. 2005 Aug;69(8):1603-5.

68 Jayasuriya WJ, Wanigatunge CA, Fernando GH, Abeytunga DT, Suresh TS. Hypoglycaemic activity of culinary Pleurotus ostreatus and P. cystidiosus mushrooms in healthy volunteers and type 2 diabetic patients on diet control and the possible mechanisms of action. Phytother Res. 2015 Feb;29(2):303-9. doi:10.1002/ptr.5255.

69 Patel, Yashvant et al. "Medicinal Properties of Pleurotus Species (Oyster Mushroom): A Review." (2012).

70 Oso, B.A. 1977. *Pleurotus tuber-regium* from Nigeria. Mycologia 69: 271-279

71 Patel, Yashvant et al. "Medicinal Properties of Pleurotus Species (Oyster Mushroom): A Review." (2012).

72 Hui-Yu Huang, Mallikarjuna Korivi, Ying-Ying Chaing, Ting-Yi Chien, Ying-Chieh Tsa. "*Pleurotus tuber-regium* Polysaccharides Attenuate Hyperglycemia and Oxidative Stress in Experimental Diabetic Rats".(2012) Hindawi, Vol 2012, Article 856381.

73 Lee YP, Tsai WC, Ko CJ, Rao YK, Yang CR, Chen DR, Yang MH, Yang CC, Tzeng YM: Anticancer effects of eleven triterpenoids derived from *Antrodia camphorata*. Anticancer Res *32*(7): 2727-2734, 2012

74 Lin, L.-H.; Chi, C.-H.; Zhang, X.-H.; Chen, Y.-J.; Wang, M.-F. Immunomodulatory Effects of Fruiting Body Extract and Solid-State-Cultivated Mycelia of *Taiwanofungus camphoratus*. Nutrients 2019, *11*, 2256.

75 Svarstad, H., Bugge, H.C. & Dhillion, S.S. From Norway to Novartis: cyclosporin from Tolypocladium inflatum in an open access bioprospecting regime. *Biodiversity and Conservation* 9, 1521–1541 (2000).

76 Hou Y, Ding X, Hou W, et al. Anti-microorganism, anti-tumor, and immune activities of a novel polysaccharide isolated from Tricholoma matsutake. *Pharmacogn Mag*. 2013;9(35):244–249. doi:10.4103/0973-1296.113278

77 Hu, Y.-N.; Sung, T.-J.; Chou, C.-H.; Liu, K.-L.; Hsieh, L.-P.; Hsieh, C.-W. Characterization and Antioxidant Activities of Yellow Strain *Flammulina velutipes* (Jinhua Mushroom) Polysaccharides and Their Effects on ROS Content in L929 Cell. *Antioxidants* 2019, *8*, 298.

78 Yuan, F.; Gao, Z.; Liu, W.; Li, H.; Zhang, Y.; Feng, Y.; Song, X.; Wang, W.; Zhang, J.; Huang, C.; Jia, L. Characterization, Antioxidant, Anti-Aging and Organ Protective Effects of Sulfated Polysaccharides from *Flammulina velutipes*. *Molecules* 2019, *24*, 3517.

79 Jayakumar T, Thomas PA, Isai M, Geraldine P. An extract of the oyster mushroom, Pleurotus ostreatus, increases catalase gene expression and reduces protein oxidation during aging in rats. Zhong Xi Yi Jie He Xue Bao. 2010 Aug;8(8):774-80.

80 Hetland G, Johnson E, Lyberg T, Kvalheim G. The Mushroom Agaricus blazei Murill Elicits Medicinal Effects on Tumor, Infection, Allergy, and Inflammation through Its Modulation of Innate Immunity and Amelioration of Th1/Th2 Imbalance and Inflammation. *Adv Pharmacol Sci*. 2011;2011:157015. doi:10.1155/2011/157015

81 Ellertsen LK, Hetland G. An extract of the medicinal mushroom Agaricus blazei Murill can protect against allergy. *Clin Mol Allergy*. 2009;7:6. Published 2009 May 5. doi:10.1186/1476-7961-7-6

82 Mizutani N, Nabe T, Shimazu M, Yoshino S, Kohno S. Effect of Ganoderma lucidum on pollen-induced biphasic nasal blockage in a guinea pig model of allergic rhinitis. Phytother Res. 2012 Mar;26(3):325-32. doi: 10.1002/ptr.3557.

83 Chen ML, Hsieh CC, Chiang BL, Lin BF. Triterpenoids and Polysaccharide Fractions of Ganoderma tsugae Exert Different Effects on Antiallergic Activities. Evid Based Complement Alternat Med. 2015;2015:754836. doi: 10.1155/2015/754836.

84 Chen YY, Lo CP, Lin CC, Hsieh YH. Effects of *Taiwanofungus camphoratus* on non-specific and specific immune activities in mice. *Mycology*. 2018;9(2):129–135. Published 2018 Feb 21. doi:10.1080/21501203.2018.1437837

85 Li IC, Lee LY, Tzeng TT, et al. Neurohealth Properties of *Hericium erinaceus* Mycelia Enriched with Erinacines. *Behav Neurol*. 2018;2018:5802634. Published 2018 May 21. doi:10.1155/2018/5802634

86 Spelman, Kevin & Sutherland, Elizabeth & Bagade, Aravind. (2017). Neurological Activity of Lion's Mane (Hericium erinaceus). Journal of Restorative Medicine. 6. 19-26. 10.14200/jrm.2017.6.0108.

87 Alresly, Zeyad. (2015). Bioactive Triterpenes from the Fungus Piptoporus betulinus. Records of Natural Products.

88 Pleszczyńska M, Lemieszek MK, Siwulski M, Wiater A, Rzeski W, Szczodrak J. Fomitopsis betulina (formerly Piptoporus betulinus): the Iceman's polypore fungus with modern biotechnological potential. *World J Microbiol Biotechnol*. 2017;33(5):83.

89 Elkhateeb, Waill & Daba, Ghoson & Elnahas, Marwa & Thomas, Paul. (2019). Anticoagulant Capacities of Some Medicinal Mushrooms. Journal of Pharmaceutical Sciences. 5. 12-16.

90 Elkhateeb, Waill & Daba, Ghoson & Elnahas, Marwa & Thomas, Paul. (2019). Anticoagulant Capacities of Some Medicinal Mushrooms. Journal of Pharmaceutical Sciences. 5. 12-16.

91 Elkhateeb, Waill & Daba, Ghoson & Elnahas, Marwa & Thomas, Paul. (2019). Anticoagulant Capacities of Some Medicinal Mushrooms. Journal of Pharmaceutical Sciences. 5. 12-16.

92 Ziaja, Katarzyna & Muszynska, Bozena & Gawalska, Alicja & Sałaciak, Kinga. (2018). Laetiporus

207

sulphureus – chemical composition and medicinal value. Acta Scientiarum Polonorum, Hortorum Cultus. 17. 87-96. 10.24326/asphc.2018.1.8.

93 Nallathamby N, Phan CW, Seow SL, et al. A Status Review of the Bioactive Activities of Tiger Milk Mushroom *Lignosus rhinocerotis* (Cooke) Ryvarden. *Front Pharmacol.* 2018;8:998. Published 2018 Jan 15. doi:10.3389/fphar.2017.00998

94 Çavuşlar Atila, Funda & Owaid, Mustafa & Shariati, Mohammad Ali. (2017). The nutritional and medical benefits of Agaricus Bisporus: A review. Journal of microbiology, biotechnology and food sciences. 7. 10.15414/jmbfs.2017/18.7.3.281-286.

95 Kosanić, Marijana & Ranković, Branislav & Stanojkovic, Tatjana. (2017). BIOACTIVITY OF EDIBLE MUSHROOM AGARICUS CAMPESTRIS.

96 Bernardshaw S, Johnson E, Hetland G. An extract of the mushroom Agaricus blazei Murill administered orally protects against systemic Streptococcus pneumoniae infection in mice. Scand J Immunol. 2005 Oct;62(4):393-8.

97 Gu YH, Leonard J. In vitro effects on proliferation, apoptosis and colony inhibition in ER-dependent and ER-independent human breast cancer cells by selected mushroom species. Oncol Rep. 2006 Feb;15(2):417-23.

98 Pleszczyńska M, Lemieszek MK, Siwulski M, Wiater A, Rzeski W, Szczodrak J. Fomitopsis betulina (formerly Piptoporus betulinus): the Iceman's polypore fungus with modern biotechnological potential. *World J Microbiol Biotechnol.* 2017;33(5):83. doi:10.1007/s11274-017-2247-0

99 Girometta, Carolina. (2018). Antimicrobial properties of Fomitopsis officinalis in the light of its bioactive metabolites: a review. Mycology. 10. 1-8. 10.1080/21501203.2018.1536680.

100 Cornell University, Cornell University Blog, Agarikon, Apr 10, 2010, https://blog.mycology.cornell.edu/2010/04/12/agarikon/

101 Girometta C. Antimicrobial properties of Fomitopsis officinalis in the light of its bioactive metabolites: a review. Mycology. 2018 Oct 25;10(1):32-39. doi:10.1080/21501203.2018.1536680.

102 Keller AC, Maillard MP, Hostettmann K. Antimicrobial steroids from the fungus Fomitopsis pinicola. Phytochemistry. 1996 Mar;41(4):1041-6.

103 Balandaykin, Mikhail & Zmitrovich, Ivan. (2015). Review on Chaga Medicinal Mushroom, Inonotus obliquus (Higher Basidiomycetes): Realm of Medicinal Applications and Approaches on Estimating its Resource Potential. International Journal of Medicinal Mushrooms. 17. 95-104. 10.1615/IntJMedMushrooms.v17.i2.10.

104 Ziaja, Katarzyna & Muszynska, Bozena & Gawalska, Alicja & Sałaciak, Kinga. (2018). Laetiporus sulphureus – chemical composition and medicinal value. Acta Scientiarum Polonorum, Hortorum Cultus. 17. 87-96. 10.24326/asphc.2018.1.8.

105 Hearst R, Nelson D, McCollum G, Millar BC, Maeda Y, Goldsmith CE, Rooney PJ,Loughrey A, Rao JR, Moore JE. An examination of antibacterial and antifungal properties of constituents of Shiitake (Lentinula edodes) and oyster (Pleurotus ostreatus) mushrooms. Complement Ther Clin Pract. 2009 Feb;15(1):5-7. doi:10.1016/j.ctcp.2008.10.002.

106 Chen W, Tan H, Liu Q, et al. A Review: The Bioactivities and Pharmacological Applications of *Phellinus linteus. Molecules.* 2019;24 (10):1888. Published 2019 May 16. doi:10.3390/molecules24101888

107 Patel, Yashvant et al. "Medicinal Properties of Pleurotus Species (Oyster Mushroom): A Review." (2012).

108 Hou Y, Ding X, Hou W, et al. Anti-microorganism, anti-tumor, and immune activities of a novel polysaccharide isolated from Tricholoma matsutake. *Pharmacogn Mag.* 2013;9(35):244–249. doi:10.4103/0973-1296.113278

109 Hakime-Silva RA, Vellosa JC, Khalil NM, Khalil OA, Brunetti IL, Oliveira OM. Chemical, enzymatic and cellular antioxidant activity studies of Agaricus blazei Murrill. An Acad Bras Cienc. 2013 Sep;85(3):1073-81. doi:10.1590/S0001-37652013005000044.

110 Çavuşlar Atila, Funda & Owaid, Mustafa & Shariati, Mohammad Ali. (2017). The nutritional and medical benefits of Agaricus Bisporus: A review. Journal of microbiology, biotechnology and food sciences. 7. 10.15414/jmbfs.2017/18.7.3.281-286.

111 Kosanić, Marijana & Ranković, Branislav & Stanojkovic, Tatjana. (2017). BIOACTIVITY OF EDIBLE MUSHROOM AGARICUS CAMPESTRIS.

112 Packialakshmi B, Sudha G and Charumathy M: Studies on phytochemical compounds and antioxidant potential of *Auricularia auricula-judae.* Int J Pharm Sci Res 2017; 8(8): 3508-15.doi: 10.13040/IJPSR.0975-8232.8(8).3508-15.

113 Yuan, Z.; Gao, Z.; Liu, W.; Li, H.; Zhang, Y.; Feng, Y.; Song, X.; Wang, W.; Zhang, J.; Huang, C.; Jia, L. Characterization, Antioxidant, Anti-Aging and Organ Protective Effects of Sulfated Polysaccharides from *Flammulina velutipes. Molecules* 2019, 24, 3517.

114 Ma, Zhao & Cui, Fangyuan & Gao, Xia & Zhang, Jianjun & Zheng, Lan & Jia, Le. (2014). Purification, characterization, antioxidant activity and anti-aging of exopolysaccharides by Flammulina velutipes SF-06. Antonie van Leeuwenhoek. 107. 10.1007/s10482-014-0305-2.

115 Rani P, Lal MR, Maheshwari U, Krishnan S. Antioxidant Potential of Lingzhi or Reishi Medicinal

Mushroom, Ganoderma lucidum (Higher Basidiomycetes) Cultivated on Artocarpus heterophyllus Sawdust Substrate in India. Int J Med Mushrooms. 2015;17(12):1171-7.

116 Balandaykin, Mikhail & Zmitrovich, Ivan. (2015). Review on Chaga Medicinal Mushroom, Inonotus obliquus (Higher Basidiomycetes): Realm of Medicinal Applications and Approaches on Estimating its Resource Potential. International Journal of Medicinal Mushrooms. 17. 95-104. 10.1615/IntJMedMushrooms.v17.i2.10.

117 Ziaja, Katarzyna & Muszynska, Bozena & Gawalska, Alicja & Sałaciak, Kinga. (2018). Laetiporus sulphureus – chemical composition and medicinal value. Acta Scientiarum Polonorum, Hortorum Cultus. 17. 87-96. 10.24326/asphc.2018.1.8.

118 Lin B, Li S. Cordyceps as an Herbal Drug. In: Benzie IFF, Wachtel-Galor S, editors. Herbal Medicine: Biomolecular and Clinical Aspects. 2nd edition. Boca Raton (FL): CRC Press/Taylor & Francis; 2011.

119 Chen W, Tan H, Liu Q, et al. A Review: The Bioactivities and Pharmacological Applications of Phellinus linteus. Molecules. 2019;24(10):1888. Published 2019 May 16. doi:10.3390/molecules24101888

120 Patel, Yashvant et al. "Medicinal Properties of Pleurotus Species (Oyster Mushroom): A Review." (2012).

121 Hsieh, Y., Wu, S., Fang, L. et al. Effects of Antrodia camphorata extracts on anti-oxidation, anti-mutagenesis and protection of DNA against hydroxyl radical damage. BMC Complement Altern Med 15, 237 (2015).

122 Brandalise F, Cesaroni V, Gregori A, et al. Dietary Supplementation of Hericium erinaceus Increases Mossy Fiber-CA3 Hippocampal Neurotransmission and Recognition Memory in Wild-Type Mice. Evid Based Complement Alternat Med. 2017;2017:3864340. doi:10.1155/2017/3864340

123 Cornell University, Cornell University Blog, Agarikon, Apr 10, 2010, https://blog.mycology.cornell.edu/2010/04/12/agarikon/

124 Bao YX, Wong CK, Li EK, Tam LS, Leung PC, Yin YB, Lam CW. Immunomodulatory effects of lingzhi and san-miao-san supplementation on patients with rheumatoid arthritis. Immunopharmacol Immunotoxicol. 2006;28(2):197-200

125 Chen W, Tan H, Liu Q, et al. A Review: The Bioactivities and Pharmacological Applications of Phellinus linteus. Molecules. 2019;24(10):1888. Published 2019 May 16. doi:10.3390/molecules24101888

126 Muhamad SA, Muhammad NS, Ismail NDA, Mohamud R, Safuan S, Nurul AA. Intranasal administration of Lignosus rhinocerotis (Cooke) Ryvarden (Tiger Milk mushroom) extract attenuates airway inflammation in murine model of allergic asthma. Exp Ther Med. 2019;17(5):3867–3876. doi:10.3892/etm.2019.7416

127 Jesenak M, Hrubisko M, Majtan J, Rennerova Z, Banovcin P. Anti-allergic effect of Pleuran (β-glucan from Pleurotus ostreatus) in children with recurrent respiratory tract infections. Phytother Res. 2014 Mar;28(3):471-4. doi: 10.1002/ptr.5020. Epub 2013 Jun 7.

128 Hetland G, Johnson E, Lyberg T, Kvalheim G. The Mushroom Agaricus blazei Murill Elicits Medicinal Effects on Tumor, Infection, Allergy, and Inflammation through Its Modulation of Innate Immunity and Amelioration of Th1/Th2 Imbalance and Inflammation. Adv Pharmacol Sci. 2011;2011:157015. doi:10.1155/2011/157015

129 Mukai H, Watanabe T, Ando M, Katsumata N. An alternative medicine, Agaricus blazei, may have induced severe hepatic dysfunction in cancer patients. Jpn J Clin Oncol. 2006 Dec;36(12):808-10.

130 Martin KR, Brophy SK. Commonly consumed and specialty dietary mushrooms reduce cellular proliferation in MCF-7 human breast cancer cells. Exp Biol Med (Maywood). 2010 Nov;235(11):1306-14. doi: 10.1258/ebm.2010.010113.

131 Çavuşlar Atila, Funda & Owaid, Mustafa & Shariati, Mohammad Ali. (2017). The nutritional and medical benefits of Agaricus Bisporus: A review. Journal of microbiology, biotechnology and food sciences. 7. 10.15414/jmbfs.2017/18.7.3.281-286.

132 Canadian Cancer Society, Toronto, Canada. https://causes.benevity.org/causes/124-118829803RR0001

133 Kosanić, Marijana & Ranković, Branislav & Stanojkovic, Tatjana. (2017). BIOACTIVITY OF EDIBLE MUSHROOM AGARICUS CAMPESTRIS.

134 Nakazato H, Koike A, Saji S, Ogawa N, Sakamoto J. Efficacy of immunochemotherapy as adjuvant treatment after curative resection of gastric cancer. Study Group of Immunochemotherapy with PSK for Gastric Cancer. Lancet. 1994 May 7;343(8906):1122-6.

135 Ohwada S, Ikeya T, Yokomori T, Kusaba T, Roppongi T, Takahashi T, Nakamura S, Kakinuma S, Iwazaki S, Ishikawa H, Kawate S, Nakajima T, Morishita Y. Adjuvant immunochemotherapy with oral Tegafur/Uracil plus PSK in patients with stage II or III colorectal cancer: a randomised controlled study. Br J Cancer. 2004 Mar8;90(5):1003-10.

136 Gu YH, Leonard J. In vitro effects on proliferation, apoptosis and colony inhibition in ER-dependent and ER-independent human breast cancer cells by selected mushroom species. Oncol Rep. 2006 Feb;15(2):417-23.

209

137 Gu YH, Leonard J. In vitro effects on proliferation, apoptosis and colony inhibition in ER-dependent and ER-independent human breast cancer cells by selected mushroom species. Oncol Rep. 2006 Feb;15(2):417-23.

138 Gu YH, Leonard J. In vitro effects on proliferation, apoptosis and colony inhibition in ER-dependent and ER-independent human breast cancer cells by selected mushroom species. Oncol Rep. 2006 Feb;15(2):417-23.

139 Zhao S, Ye G, Fu G, Cheng JX, Yang BB, Peng C. Ganoderma lucidum exerts anti-tumor effects on ovarian cancer cells and enhances their sensitivity to cisplatin. Int J Oncol. 2011 May;38(5):1319-27. doi: 10.3892/ijo.2011.965.

140 Gao Y, Zhou S, Jiang W, Huang M, Dai X. Effects of ganopoly (a Ganoderma lucidum polysaccharide extract) on the immune functions in advanced-stage cancer patients. Immunol Invest. 2003 Aug;32(3):201-15.

141 Wang CZ, Basila D, Aung HH, Mehendale SR, Chang WT, McEntee E, Guan X, Yuan CS. Effects of ganoderma lucidum extract on chemotherapy-induced nausea and vomiting in a rat model. Am J Chin Med. 2005;33(5):807-15.

142 Kim KC, Jun HJ, Kim JS, Kim IG. Enhancement of radiation response with combined Ganoderma lucidum and Duchesnea chrysantha extracts in human leukemia HL-60 cells. Int J Mol Med. 2008 Apr;21(4):489-98.

143 Chen NH, Liu JW, Zhong JJ. Ganoderic acid Me inhibits tumor invasion through down-regulating matrix metalloproteinases 2/9 gene expression. J Pharmacol Sci. 2008 Oct;108(2):212-6.

144 Gill SK, Rieder MJ. Toxicity of a traditional Chinese medicine, Ganoderma lucidum, in children with cancer. Can J Clin Pharmacol. 2008 Summer;15(2):e275-85. Epub 2008 Jul 4.

145 Jin X, Ruiz Beguerie J, Sze DM, Chan GC. Ganoderma lucidum (Reishi mushroom) for cancer treatment. Cochrane Database Syst Rev. 2012 Jun 13;(6):CD007731. doi: 10.1002/14651858.CD007731.pub2. Review. Update in: Cochrane Database Syst Rev. 2016;4:CD007731.

146 Kodama N, Komuta K, Nanba H. Can maitake MD-fraction aid cancer patients? Altern Med Rev. 2002 Jun;7(3):236-9

147 Masuda Y, Ito K, Konishi M, Nanba H. A polysaccharide extracted from Grifola frondosa enhances the anti-tumor activity of bone marrow-derived dendritic cell-based immunotherapy against murine colon cancer. Cancer Immunol Immunother. 2010 Oct;59(10):1531-41. doi: 10.1007/s00262-010-0880-7.

148 Martin KR, Brophy SK. Commonly consumed and specialty dietary mushrooms reduce cellular proliferation in MCF-7 human breast cancer cells. Exp Biol Med (Maywood). 2010 Nov;235(11):1306-14. doi: 10.1258/ebm.2010.010113

149 Zhang Y, Sun D, Meng Q, Guo W, Chen Q, Zhang Y. Grifola frondosa polysaccharides induce breast cancer cell apoptosis via the mitochondrial-dependent apoptotic pathway. Int J Mol Med. 2017 Oct;40(4):1089-1095. doi: 10.3892/ijmm.2017.3081.

150 Pleszczyńska M, Wiater A, Siwulski M, et al. Cultivation and utility of Piptoporus betulinus fruiting bodies as a source of anticancer agents. World J Microbiol Biotechnol. 2016;32(9):151. doi:10.1007/s11274-016-2114-4

151 Grienke, Ulrike & Zöll, Margit & Peintner, Ursula & Rollinger, Judith. (2014). European medicinal polypores – A modern view on traditional uses. Journal of Ethnopharmacology. 10.1016/j.jep.2014.04.030.

152 Rogers, Robert. (2014). Three Under-utilized Medicinal Polypores. Journal of American Herbalists Guild. Vol 12. No 2.

153 Rogers, Robert. (2014). Three Under-utilized Medicinal Polypores. Journal of American Herbalists Guild. Vol 12. No 2.

154 Balandaykin ME, Zmitrovich IV. Review on Chaga Medicinal Mushroom, Inonotus obliquus (Higher Basidiomycetes): Realm of Medicinal Applications and Approaches on Estimating its Resource Potential. Int J Med Mushrooms. 2015;17(2):95-104.

155 Ziaja, Katarzyna & Muszynska, Bozena & Gawalska, Alicja & Sałaciak, Kinga. (2018). Laetiporus sulphureus – chemical composition and medicinal value. Acta Scientiarum Polonorum, Hortorum Cultus. 17. 87-96. 10.24326/asphc.2018.1.8.

156 Memorial Sloan Kettering Cancer Center. Clinical Summary, AHCC https://www.mskcc.org/cancer-care/integrative-medicine/herbs/ahcc

157 Matsui Y, Uhara J, Satoi S, Kaibori M, Yamada H, Kitade H, Imamura A, Takai S, Kawaguchi Y, Kwon AH, Kamiyama Y. Improved prognosis of postoperative hepatocellular carcinoma patients when treated with functional foods: a prospective cohort study. J Hepatol. 2002 Jul;37(1):78-86.

158 Nallathamby N, Phan CW, Seow SL, et al. A Status Review of the Bioactive Activities of Tiger Milk Mushroom Lignosus rhinocerotis (Cooke) Ryvarden. Front Pharmacol. 2018;8:998. Published 2018 Jan 15. doi:10.3389/fphar.2017.00998

159 Nakamura K, Yamaguchi Y, Kagota S, Kwon YM, Shinozuka K, Kunitomo M. Inhibitory effect of Cordyceps sinensis on spontaneous liver metastasis of Lewis lung carcinoma and B16 melanoma

210

cells in syngeneic mice. Jpn J Pharmacol. 1999 Mar;79(3):335-41.

160 Wu WC, Hsiao JR, Lian YY, Lin CY, Huang BM. The apoptotic effect of cordycepin on human OEC-M1 oral cancer cell line. Cancer Chemother Pharmacol. 2007 Jun;60(1):103-11. Epub 2006 Oct 10.

161 Liu WC, Wang SC, Tsai ML, Chen MC, Wang YC, Hong JH, McBride WH, Chiang CS. Protection against radiation-induced bone marrow and intestinal injuries by Cordyceps sinensis, a Chinese herbal medicine. Radiat Res. 2006 Dec;166(6):900-7.

162 Ji NF, Yao LS, Li Y, He W, Yi KS, Huang M. Polysaccharide of Cordyceps sinensis enhances cisplatin cytotoxicity in non-small cell lung cancer H157 cell line. Integr Cancer Ther. 2011 Dec;10(4):359-67. doi: 10.1177/1534735410392573.Epub 2011 Mar 7.

163 Chen W, Tan H, Liu Q, et al. A Review: The Bioactivities and Pharmacological Applications of *Phellinus linteus*. *Molecules*. 2019;24(10):1888. Published 2019 May 16. doi:10.3390/molecules24101888

164 Sliva D. Medicinal mushroom Phellinus linteus as an alternative cancer therapy. *Exp Ther Med*. 2010;1(3):407–411. doi:10.3892/etm_00000063

165 Konno S, Chu K, Feuer N, Phillips J, Choudhury M. Potent Anticancer Effects of Bioactive Mushroom Extracts (Phellinus linteus) on a Variety of Human Cancer Cells. J Clin Med Res. 2015 Feb;7(2):76-82. doi: 10.14740/jocmr1996w.

166 Shlyakhovenko V, Kosak V, Olishevsky S. Application of DNA from mushroom Pleurotus ostreatus for cancer biotherapy: a pilot study. Exp Oncol. 2006 Jun;28(2):132-5.

167 Jedinak, Andrej & Sliva, Daniel. (2009). Pleurotus ostreatus inhibits proliferation of human breast and colon cancer cells through p53-dependent as well as p53-independent pathway. International journal of oncology. 33. 1307-13.

168 Martin KR, Brophy SK. Commonly consumed and specialty dietary mushrooms reduce cellular proliferation in MCF-7 human breast cancer cells. Exp Biol Med (Maywood). 2010 Nov;235(11):1306-14. doi: 10.1258/ebm.2010.010113.

169 Jedinak A, Dudhgaonkar S, Jiang J, Sandusky G, Sliva D. Pleurotus ostreatus inhibits colitis-related colon carcinogenesis in mice. Int J Mol Med. 2010 Nov;26(5):643-50.

170 Lin LT, Tai CJ, Su CH, Chang FM, Choong CY, Wang CK, Tai CJ. The Ethanolic Extract of Taiwanofungus camphoratus (Antrodia camphorata) Induces Cell Cycle Arrest and Enhances Cytotoxicity of Cisplatin and Doxorubicin on Human Hepatocellular Carcinoma Cells. Biomed Res Int. 2015;2015:415269. doi: 10.1155/2015/415269. Epub 2015 Oct 18.

171 Lee YP, Tsai WC, Ko CJ, Rao YK, Yang CR, Chen DR, Yang MH, Yang CC, Tzeng YM: Anticancer effects of eleven triterpenoids derived from *Antrodia camphorata*. Anticancer Res *32*(7): 2727-2734, 2012.

172 Wang, G.-J., Huang, Y.-J., Chen, D.-H. and Lin, Y.-L. (2009), *Ganoderma lucidum* extract attenuates the proliferation of hepatic stellate cells by blocking the PDGF receptor. Phytother. Res., 23: 833-839. doi:10.1002/ptr.2687

173 Zhu, J S., et al. "The Scientific Rediscovery of a Precious Ancient Chinese Herbal Regimen: Cordyceps Sinensis: Part II." *Journal of Alternative and Complementary Medicine (New York, N.Y.)*, vol. 4, no. 4, 1998, pp. 429-57.

174 Thangthaeng N, Miller MG, Gomes SM, Shukitt-Hale B. Daily supplementation with mushroom (Agaricus bisporus) improves balance and working memory in aged rats. Nutr Res. 2015 Dec;35(12):1079-84. doi: 10.1016/j.nutres.2015.09.012.

175 Spelman, Kevin & Sutherland, Elizabeth & Bagade, Aravind. (2017). Neurological Activity of Lion's Mane (Hericium erinaceus). Journal of Restorative Medicine. 6. 19-26. 10.14200/jrm.2017.6.0108.

176 Yang, Wenjian & Fang, Yong & Liang, Jin & Hu, Qiuhui. (2011). Optimization of ultrasonic extraction of Flammulina velutipes polysaccharides and evaluation of its acetylcholinesterase inhibitory activity. Food Research International. 44. 1269-1275. 10.1016/j.foodres.2010.11.027.

177 Li IC, Lee LY, Tzeng TT, et al. Neurohealth Properties of *Hericium erinaceus* Mycelia Enriched with Erinacines. *Behav Neurol*. 2018;2018:5802634. Published 2018 May 21. doi:10.1155/2018/5802634

178 Nagano M, Shimizu K, Kondo R, Hayashi C, Sato D, Kitagawa K, Ohnuki K. Reduction of depression and anxiety by 4 weeks Hericium erinaceus intake. Biomed Res. 2010 Aug;31(4):231-7.

179 Qin DW, Han C. Medicinal and edible fungi as an alternative medicine for treating age-related disease. Evid Based Complement Alternat Med. 2014;2014:638561. doi: 10.1155/2014/638561. Epub 2014 Apr 29.

180 Xian HM, Che H, Qin Y, Yang F, Meng SY, Li XG, Bai YL, Wang LH. Coriolus versicolor aqueous extract ameliorates insulin resistance with PI3K/Akt and p38 MAPK signaling pathways involved in diabetic skeletal muscle. Phytother Res. 2018 Mar;32(3):551-560. doi: 10.1002/ptr.6007.

181 Wang Y, Li H, Li Y, Zhao Y, Xiong F, Liu Y, Xue H, Yang Z, Ni S, Sahil A, Che H, Wang L. Coriolus versicolor alleviates diabetic cardiomyopathy by inhibiting cardiac fibrosis and NLRP3 inflammasome activation. Phytother Res. 2019 Oct;33(10):2737-2748. doi: 10.1002/ptr.6448. Epub 2019 Jul 23.

182 Rogers, Robert. (2014). Three Under-utilized Medicinal Polypores. Journal of American Herbalists Guild. Vol 12. No 2.

211

183 Horio H, Ohtsuru M. Maitake (Grifola frondosa) improve glucose tolerance of experimental diabetic rats. J Nutr Sci Vitaminol (Tokyo)

184 Liang B, Guo Z, Xie F, Zhao A. Antihyperglycemic and antihyperlipidemic activities of aqueous extract of Hericium erinaceus in experimental diabetic rats. BMC Complement Altern Med. 2013;13:253. Published 2013 Oct 3. doi:10.1186/1472-6882-13-253

185 Yi Z, Shao-Long Y, Ai-Hong W, et al. Protective Effect of Ethanol Extracts of Hericium erinaceus on Alloxan-Induced Diabetic Neuropathic Pain in Rats. Evid Based Complement Alternat Med. 2015;2015:595480. doi:10.1155/2015/595480

186 Balandaykin, Mikhail & Zmitrovich, Ivan. (2015). Review on Chaga Medicinal Mushroom, Inonotus obliquus (Higher Basidiomycetes): Realm of Medicinal Applications and Approaches on Estimating its Resource Potential. International Journal of Medicinal Mushrooms. 17. 95-104. 10.1615/IntJMedMushrooms.v17.i2.10.

187 Jiri, Patocka. "Will the Sulphur Polypore (laetiporus Sulphureus) Become a New Functional Food?" Global Journal of Medical and Clinical Case Reports 6.1 (2019): 006–009.

188 Lo HC, Hsu TH, Tu ST, Lin KC. Anti-hyperglycemic activity of natural and fermented Cordyceps sinensis in rats with diabetes induced by nicotinamide and streptozotocin. Am J Chin Med. 2006;34(5):819-32

189 Shi B, Wang Z, Jin H, Chen YW, Wang Q, Qian Y. Immunoregulatory Cordyceps sinensis increases regulatory T cells to Th17 cell ratio and delays diabetes in NOD mice. Int Immunopharmacol. 2009 May;9(5):582-6.

190 Kai Z, Yongjian L, Sheng G, Yu L. Effect of Dongchongxiacao (Cordyceps) therapy on contrast-induced nephropathy in patients with type 2 diabetes and renal insufficiency undergoing coronary angiography. J Tradit Chin Med. 2015 Aug;35(4):422-7.

191 Zhu, J S., et al. "The Scientific Rediscovery of a Precious Ancient Chinese Herbal Regimen: Cordyceps Sinensis: Part II." Journal of Alternative and Complementary Medicine (New York, N.Y.), vol. 4, no. 4, 1998, pp. 429-57.

192 Chen W, Tan H, Liu Q, et al. A Review: The Bioactivities and Pharmacological Applications of Phellinus linteus. Molecules. 2019;24(10):1888. Published 2019 May 16. doi:10.3390/molecules24101888

193 Jayasuriya WJ, Wanigatunge CA, Fernando GH, Abeytunga DT, Suresh TS. Hypoglycaemic activity of culinary Pleurotus ostreatus and P. cystidiosus mushrooms in healthy volunteers and type 2 diabetic patients on diet control and the possible mechanisms of action. Phytother Res. 2015 Feb;29(2):303-9. doi:10.1002/ptr.5255. Epub 2014 Nov 8.

194 Chorváthová V, Bobek P, Ginter E, Klvanová J. Effect of the oyster fungus on glycaemia and cholesterolaemia in rats with insulin-dependent diabetes. Physiol Res. 1993;42(3):175-9.

195 Huang, Hui-Yu & Korivi, Mallikarjuna & Chaing, Ying-Ying & Chien, Ting-Yi & Ying Chieh, Tsai. (2012). Pleurotus tuber-regium Polysaccharides Attenuate Hyperglycemia and Oxidative Stress in Experimental Diabetic Rats. Evidence-based complementary and alternative medicine : eCAM. 2012. 856381. 10.1155/2012/856381.

196 Vong CT, Tseng HHL, Kwan YW, Lee SM-Y and Hoi MPM (2016) Antrodia camphorata Increases Insulin Secretion and Protects from Apoptosis in MIN6 Cells. Front. Pharmacol. 7:67. doi: 10.3389/fphar.2016.00067

197 Chen S, Li Z, Krochmal R, Abrazado M, Kim W, Cooper CB. Effect of Cs-4 (Cordyceps sinensis) on exercise performance in healthy older subjects: a double-blind, placebo-controlled trial. J Altern Complement Med. 2010 May;16(5):585-90. doi: 10.1089/acm.2009.0226.

198 Parcell AC, Smith JM, Schulthies SS, Myrer JW, Fellingham G. Cordyceps Sinensis (CordyMax Cs-4) supplementation does not improve endurance exercise performance. Int J Sport Nutr Exerc Metab. 2004 Apr;14(2):236-42.

199 Tang, Wenbo & Gao, Yihuai & Chen, Guoliang & Gao, He & Dai, Xihu & Ye, Jinxian & Chan, Eli & Huang, Min & Zhou, Shufeng. (2005). A Randomized, Double-Blind and Placebo-Controlled Study of a Ganoderma lucidum Polysaccharide Extract in Neurasthenia. Journal of medicinal food. 8. 53-8. 10.1089/jmf.2005.8.53.

200 Zhu, J S., et al. "The Scientific Rediscovery of a Precious Ancient Chinese Herbal Regimen: Cordyceps Sinensis: Part II." Journal of Alternative and Complementary Medicine (New York, N.Y.), vol. 4, no. 4, 1998, pp. 429-57.

201 Lin B, Li S. Cordyceps as an Herbal Drug. In: Benzie IFF, Wachtel-Galor S, editors. Herbal Medicine: Biomolecular and Clinical Aspects. 2nd edition. Boca Raton (FL): CRC Press/Taylor & Francis; 2011.

202 https://patents.google.com/patent/US7468392

203 Patel, Yashvant et al. "Medicinal Properties of Pleurotus Species (Oyster Mushroom): A Review." (2012).

204 Hess, J.; Wang, Q.; Gould, T.; Slavin, J. Impact of Agaricus bisporus Mushroom Consumption on Gut Health Markers in Healthy Adults. Nutrients 2018, 10, 1402.

205 Solano-Aguilar, Gloria & Jang, Saebyeol & Lakshman, Sukla & Gupta, Richi & Beshah, Ethiopia &

Sikaroodi, Masoumeh & Vinyard, Bryan & Molokin, Aleksey & Gillevet, Patrick & Urban, Joseph. (2018). The Effect of Dietary Mushroom Agaricus bisporus on Intestinal Microbiota Composition and Host Immunological Function. Nutrients. 10. 1721. 10.3390/nu10111721.

206 Wong JY, Abdulla MA, Raman J, et al. Gastroprotective Effects of Lion's Mane Mushroom Hericium erinaceus (Bull.:Fr.) Pers. (Aphyllophoromycetideae) Extract against Ethanol-Induced Ulcer in Rats. *Evid Based Complement Alternat Med.* 2013;2013:492976. doi:10.1155/2013/492976

207 Lin B, Li S. Cordyceps as an Herbal Drug. In: Benzie IFF, Wachtel-Galor S, editors. Herbal Medicine: Biomolecular and Clinical Aspects. 2nd edition. Boca Raton (FL): CRC Press/Taylor & Francis; 2011. Chapter 5.

208 Zhu, J S., et al. "The Scientific Rediscovery of a Precious Ancient Chinese Herbal Regimen: Cordyceps Sinensis: Part II." *Journal of Alternative and Complementary Medicine (New York, N.Y.),* vol. 4, no. 4, 1998, pp. 429-57.

209 Li IC, Lee LY, Tzeng TT, et al. Neurohealth Properties of *Hericium erinaceus* Mycelia Enriched with Erinacines. *Behav Neurol.* 2018;2018:5802634. Published 2018 May 21. doi:10.1155/2018/5802634

210 Grienke U, Zöll M, Peintner U, Rollinger JM. European medicinal polypores--a modern view on traditional uses. J Ethnopharmacol. 2014 Jul 3;154(3):564-83. doi:10.1016/j.jep.2014.04.030. Epub 2014 Apr 28.

211 Hsu CH, Hwang KC, Chiang YH, Chou P. The mushroom Agaricus blazei Murill extract normalizes liver function in patients with chronic hepatitis B. J Altern Complement Med. 2008 Apr;14(3):299-301. doi: 10.1089/acm.2006.6344.

212 Qin DW, Han C. Medicinal and edible fungi as an alternative medicine for treating age-related disease. Evid Based Complement Alternat Med. 2014;2014:638561. doi: 10.1155/2014/638561. Epub 2014 Apr 29.

213 Zhu, J S., et al. "The Scientific Rediscovery of a Precious Ancient Chinese Herbal Regimen: Cordyceps Sinensis: Part II." *Journal of Alternative and Complementary Medicine (New York, N.Y.),* vol. 4, no. 4, 1998, pp. 429-57.

214 Chen W, Tan H, Liu Q, et al. A Review: The Bioactivities and Pharmacological Applications of *Phellinus linteus. Molecules.* 2019;24(10):1888. Published 2019 May 16. doi:10.3390/molecules24101888

215 I.-Hung Lee, Ray-Ling Huang, Chi-Ting Chen, Hsiao-Chuan Chen, Wen-Chi Hsu, Mei-Kuang Lu, *Antrodia camphorata* polysaccharides exhibit anti-hepatitis B virus effects, *FEMS Microbiology Letters,* Volume 209, Issue 1, March 2002, Pages 63–67,

216 Shibnev, V.A. & Mishin, Dmitriy & Garaev, Timur & Finogenova, N.P. & Botikov, A.G. & Deryabin, Petr. (2011). Antiviral Activity of Inonotus Obliquus Fungus Extract towards Infection Caused by Hepatitis C Virus in Cell Cultures. Bulletin of experimental biology and medicine. 151. 612-4. 10.1007/s10517-011-1395-8.

217 Çavuşlar Atila, Funda & Owaid, Mustafa & Shariati, Mohammad Ali. (2017). The nutritional and medical benefits of Agaricus Bisporus: A review. Journal of microbiology, biotechnology and food sciences. 7. 10.15414/jmbfs.2017/18.7.3.281-286.

218 Sękara, Agnieszka & Kalisz, Andrzej & Grabowska, Aneta & Siwulski, Marek. (2015). Auricularia spp. - mushrooms as Novel Food and therapeutic agents - a review. Sydowia -Horn-. 67. 1-10. 10.12905/0380.sydowia67-2015-0001.

219 Yeh MY, Ko WC, Lin LY. Hypolipidemic and antioxidant activity of enoki mushrooms (Flammulina velutipes). *Biomed Res Int.* 2014;2014:352385. doi:10.1155/2014/352385

220 Balandaykin, Mikhail & Zmitrovich, Ivan. (2015). Review on Chaga Medicinal Mushroom, Inonotus obliquus (Higher Basidiomycetes): Realm of Medicinal Applications and Approaches on Estimating its Resource Potential. International Journal of Medicinal Mushrooms. 17. 95-104. 10.1615/IntJMedMushrooms.v17.i2.10.

221 Ziaja, Katarzyna & Muszynska, Bozena & Gawalska, Alicja & Sałaciak, Kinga. (2018). Laetiporus sulphureus – chemical composition and medicinal value. Acta Scientiarum Polonorum, Hortorum Cultus. 17. 87-96. 10.24326/asphc.2018.1.8.

222 Yang H, Hwang I, Kim S, Hong EJ, Jeung EB. Lentinus edodes promotes fat removal in hypercholesterolemic mice. Exp Ther Med. 2013 Dec;6(6):1409-1413.

223 Zhu, J S., et al. "The Scientific Rediscovery of a Precious Ancient Chinese Herbal Regimen: Cordyceps Sinensis: Part II." *Journal of Alternative and Complementary Medicine (New York, N.Y.),* vol. 4, no. 4, 1998, pp. 429-57.

224 Bobek P, Ozdín L, Kuniak L. Effect of oyster mushroom (Pleurotus Ostreatus) and its ethanolic extract in diet on absorption and turnover of cholesterol in hypercholesterolemic rat. Nahrung. 1996 Aug;40(4):222-4

225 Hossain S, Hashimoto M, Choudhury EK, Alam N, Hussain S, Hasan M, Choudhury SK, Mahmud I. Dietary mushroom (Pleurotus ostreatus) ameliorates atherogenic lipid in hypercholesterolaemic rats. Clin Exp Pharmacol Physiol. 2003 Jul;30(7):470-5.

226 Alarcón, Julio & Aguila, Sergio & Arancibia, Patricia & Fuentes, Oscar & Zamorano-Ponce, Enrique & Hernández, Margarita. (2003). Production and Purification of Statins from Pleurotus ostreatus

213

(Basidiomycetes) Strains. Zeitschrift für Naturforschung. C, Journal of biosciences. 58. 62-4. 10.1515/znc-2003-1-211.

227 Lovastatin, Wikipedia https://en.wikipedia.org/wiki/Lovastatin

228 Rogers, Robert. (2014). Three Under-utilized Medicinal Polypores. Journal of American Herbalists Guild. Vol 12. No 2.

229 Shibnev VA, Garaev TM, Finogenova MP, Kalnina LB, Nosik DN. [Antiviral activity of aqueous extracts of the birch fungus Inonotus obliquus on the human immunodeficiency virus]. Vopr Virusol. 2015;60(2):35-8.

230 Khatua, Somanjana et al. "Laetiporus sulphureus (Bull.: Fr.) Murr. as Food as Medicine." (2017).

231 Pang, Xiubing & Yao, Wenbing & Yang, Xiaobing & Xie, Chen & Liu, Dong & Zhang, Jian & Gao, Xiangdong. (2007). Purification, characterization and biological activity on hepatocytes of a polysaccharide from Flammulina velutipes mycelium. Carbohydrate Polymers. 70. 291-297. 10.1016/j.carbpol.2007.04.010.

232 Elkhateeb, Waill & Daba, Ghoson & Elnahas, Marwa & Thomas, Paul. (2019). Anticoagulant Capacities of Some Medicinal Mushrooms. Journal of Pharmaceutical Sciences. 5. 12-16.

233 Hagiwara SY, Takahashi M, Shen Y, Kaihou S, Tomiyama T, Yazawa M, Tamai Y, Sin Y, Kazusaka A, Terazawa M. A phytochemical in the edible Tamogi-take mushroom (Pleurotus cornucopiae), D-mannitol, inhibits ACE activity and lowers the blood pressure of spontaneously hypertensive rats. Biosci Biotechnol Biochem. 2005 Aug;69(8):1603-5.

234 Yuan, Z et al. "Hypoglycemic effect of water-soluble polysaccharide from Auricularia auricula-judae Quel. on genetically diabetic KK-Ay mice." Bioscience, biotechnology, and biochemistry 62 10 (1998): 1898-903.

235 Cha, J.Y. & Jun, B.S. & Kim, J.W. & Park, S.H. & Lee, C.H. & Cho, Y.S.. (2006). Hypoglycemic effects of fermented chaga mushroom (Inonotus obliquus) in the diabetic Otsuka Long-Evans Tokushima Fatty (OLETF) rat. Food science and biotechnology. 15. 739-745.

236 Saleh MH, Rashedi I, Keating A. Immunomodulatory Properties of Coriolus versicolor: The Role of Polysaccharopeptide. Front Immunol. 2017;8:1087. Published 2017 Sep 6. doi:10.3389/fimmu.2017.01087

237 Jeurink PV, Noguera CL, Savelkoul HF, Wichers HJ. Immunomodulatory capacity of fungal proteins on the cytokine production of human peripheral blood mononuclear cells. Int Immunopharmacol. 2008 Aug;8(8):1124-33. doi: 10.1016/j.intimp.2008.04.004.

238 Jeurink PV, Noguera CL, Savelkoul HF, Wichers HJ. Immunomodulatory capacity of fungal proteins on the cytokine production of human peripheral blood mononuclear cells. Int Immunopharmacol. 2008 Aug;8(8):1124-33. doi: 10.1016/j.intimp.2008.04.004.

239 Yin H, Wang Y, Wang Y, Chen T, Tang H, Wang M. Purification, characterization and immuno-modulating properties of polysaccharides isolated from Flammulina velutipes mycelium. Am J Chin Med. 2010;38(1):191-204.

240 Lull C, Wichers HJ, Savelkoul HF. Antiinflammatory and immunomodulating properties of fungal metabolites. Mediators Inflamm. 2005;2005(2):63–80. doi:10.1155/MI.2005.63

241 Balandaykin, Mikhail & Zmitrovich, Ivan. (2015). Review on Chaga Medicinal Mushroom, Inonotus obliquus (Higher Basidiomycetes): Realm of Medicinal Applications and Approaches on Estimating its Resource Potential. International Journal of Medicinal Mushrooms. 17. 95-104. 10.1615/IntJMedMushrooms.v17.i2.10.

242 Dai X, Stanilka JM, Rowe CA, Esteves EA, Nieves C Jr, Spaiser SJ, Christman MC, Langkamp-Henken B, Percival SS. Consuming Lentinula edodes (Shiitake) Mushrooms Daily Improves Human Immunity: A Randomized Dietary Intervention in Healthy Young Adults. J Am Coll Nutr. 2015;34(6):478-87. doi: 10.1080/07315724.2014.950391.

243 Nallathamby N, Phan CW, Seow SL, et al. A Status Review of the Bioactive Activities of Tiger Milk Mushroom Lignosus rhinocerotis (Cooke) Ryvarden. Front Pharmacol. 2018;8:998. Published 2018 Jan 15. doi:10.3389/fphar.2017.00998

244 Chen W, Tan H, Liu Q, et al. A Review: The Bioactivities and Pharmacological Applications of Phellinus linteus. Molecules. 2019;24(10):1888. Published 2019 May 16. doi:10.3390/molecules24101888

245 Jung, S., Jung, E., Choi, E. et al. Immunomodulatory effects of a mycelium extract of Cordyceps (Paecilomyces hepiali; CBG-CS-2): a randomized and double-blind clinical trial. BMC Complement Altern Med 19, 77 (2019).

246 Lin B, Li S. Cordyceps as an Herbal Drug. In: Benzie IFF, Wachtel-Galor S, editors. Herbal Medicine: Biomolecular and Clinical Aspects. 2nd edition. Boca Raton (FL): CRC Press/Taylor & Francis; 2011. Chapter 5.

247 Chen YY, Lo CP, Lin CC, Hsieh YH. Effects of Taiwanofungus camphoratus on non-specific and specific immune activities in mice. Mycology. 2018;9(2):129–135. Published 2018 Feb 21. doi:10.1080/21501203.2018.1437837

248 Hou Y, Ding X, Hou W, et al. Anti-microorganism, anti-tumor, and immune activities of a novel polysaccharide isolated from Tricholoma matsutake. Pharmacogn Mag. 2013;9(35):244–249.

doi:10.4103/0973-1296.113278

249 Hetland G, Johnson E, Lyberg T, Kvalheim G. The Mushroom Agaricus blazei Murill Elicits Medicinal Effects on Tumor, Infection, Allergy, and Inflammation through Its Modulation of Innate Immunity and Amelioration of Th1/Th2 Imbalance and Inflammation. *Adv Pharmacol Sci.* 2011;2011:157015. doi:10.1155/2011/157015

250 Sękara, Agnieszka & Kalisz, Andrzej & Grabowska, Aneta & Siwulski, Marek. (2015). Auricularia spp. - mushrooms as Novel Food and therapeutic agents - a review. Sydowia -Horn-. 67. 1-10. 10.12905/0380.sydowia67-2015-0001.

251 Zhuan-Yun LI, Xue-Ping Y, Bin L, et al. *Auricularia auricular-judae* polysaccharide attenuates lipopolysaccharide-induced acute lung injury by inhibiting oxidative stress and inflammation. *Biomed Rep.* 2015;3(4):478–482. doi:10.3892/br.2015.470

252 Gunawardena, Dhanushka & Bennett, Louise & Shanmugam, Kirubakaran & King, Kerryn & Williams, Roderick & Zabaras, Dimitrios & Head, Richard & Ooi, Lezanne & Gyengési, Erika & Muench, Gerald. (2014). Anti-inflammatory effects of five commercially available mushroom species determined in lipopolysaccharide and interferon-γ activated murine macrophages. Food chemistry. 148C. 92-96. 10.1016/j.foodchem.2013.10.015.

253 Rogers, Robert. (2014). Three Under-utilized Medicinal Polypores. Journal of American Herbalists Guild. Vol 12. No 2.

254 Kamo, Tsunashi et al. "Anti-inflammatory lanostane-type triterpene acids from Piptoporus betulinus." *Journal of natural products* 66 8 (2003): 1104-6 .

255 Wong JY, Abdulla MA, Raman J, et al. Gastroprotective Effects of Lion's Mane Mushroom Hericium erinaceus (Bull.:Fr.) Pers. (Aphyllophoromycetideae) Extract against Ethanol-Induced Ulcer in Rats. *Evid Based Complement Alternat Med.* 2013;2013:492976. doi:10.1155/2013/492976

256 Mori K, Ouchi K, Hirasawa N. The Anti-Inflammatory Effects of Lion's Mane Culinary-Medicinal Mushroom, Hericium erinaceus (Higher Basidiomycetes) in a Coculture System of 3T3-L1 Adipocytes and RAW264 Macrophages. Int J Med Mushrooms. 2015;17(7):609-18.

257 Patocka J (2019) Will the sulphur polypore (*laetiporus sulphureus*) become a new functional food?. Glob J Medical Clin Case Rep 6(1): 006-009. DOI: 10.17352/2455-5282.000068

258 Lee, Sookshien & Tan, Nget & Fung, Shin & Sim, Si Mui & Tan, Chon-Seng & Ng, Szu. (2014). Anti-inflammatory effect of the sclerotium of Lignosus rhinocerotis (Cooke) Ryvarden, the Tiger Milk mushroom. BMC complementary and alternative medicine. 14. 359. 10.1186/1472-6882-14-359.

259 Chen W, Tan H, Liu Q, et al. A Review: The Bioactivities and Pharmacological Applications of *Phellinus linteus. Molecules.* 2019;24(10):1888. Published 2019 May 16. doi:10.3390/molecules24101888

260 Cui XY, Cui SY, Zhang J, Wang ZJ, Yu B, Sheng ZF, Zhang XQ, Zhang YH. Extract of Ganoderma lucidum prolongs sleep time in rats. J Ethnopharmacol. 2012 Feb 15;139(3):796-800. doi: 10.1016/j.jep.2011.12.020.

261 Lee JS, Park SY, Thapa D, Choi MK, Chung IM, Park YJ, Yong CS, Choi HG, Kim JA. Grifola frondosa water extract alleviates intestinal inflammation by suppressing TNF-alpha production and its signaling. Exp Mol Med. 2010 Feb 28;42(2):143-54. doi: 10.3858/emm.2010.42.2.016.

262 Qin M, Geng Y, Lu Z, Xu H, Shi JS, Xu X, Xu ZH. Anti-Inflammatory Effects of Ethanol Extract of Lion's Mane Medicinal Mushroom, Hericium erinaceus (Agaricomycetes), in Mice with Ulcerative Colitis. Int J Med Mushrooms. 2016;18(3):227-34. doi: 10.1615/IntJMedMushrooms.v18.i3.50.

263 Wong JY, Abdulla MA, Raman J, et al. Gastroprotective Effects of Lion's Mane Mushroom Hericium erinaceus (Bull.:Fr.) Pers. (Aphyllophoromycetideae) Extract against Ethanol-Induced Ulcer in Rats. *Evid Based Complement Alternat Med.* 2013;2013:492976. doi:10.1155/2013/492976

264 Hong T, Zhang M, Fan J. Cordyceps sinensis (a traditional Chinese medicine) for kidney transplant recipients. Cochrane Database Syst Rev. 2015 Oct 12;(10):CD009698. doi: 10.1002/14651858.CD009698.pub2. Review.

265 Bobek P, Galbavy S. Effect of pleuran (beta-glucan from Pleurotus ostreatus) on the antioxidant status of the organism and on dimethylhydrazine-induced precancerous lesions in rat colon. Br J Biomed Sci. 2001;58(3):164-8.

266 Zhu, Jia-Shi & Halpern, Georges & Jones, Kenneth. (1998). The Scientific Rediscovery of a Precious Ancient Chinese Herbal Regimen: Cordyceps sinensis Part II. Journal of alternative and complementary medicine (New York, N.Y.). 4. 429-57. 10.1089/acm.1998.4.429.

267 Lin B, Li S. Cordyceps as an Herbal Drug. In: Benzie IFF, Wachtel-Galor S, editors. Herbal Medicine: Biomolecular and Clinical Aspects. 2nd edition. Boca Raton (FL): CRC Press/Taylor & Francis; 2011. Chapter 5.

268 Panda AK, Swain KC. Traditional uses and medicinal potential of Cordyceps sinensis of Sikkim. *J Ayurveda Integr Med.* 2011;2(1):9–13. doi:10.4103/0975-9476.78183

269 Hobbs, Christopher. Medicinal Mushrooms III (1998), www.christopherhobbs.com

270 Wang, G.-J., Huang, Y.-J., Chen, D.-H. and Lin, Y.-L. (2009), *Ganoderma lucidum* extract attenuates the proliferation of hepatic stellate cells by blocking the PDGF receptor. Phytother. Res., 23: 833-839. doi:10.1002/ptr.2687

271 Khatua, Somanjana et al. "Laetiporus sulphureus (Bull.: Fr.) Murr. as Food as Medicine." (2017).
272 Nallathamby N, Phan CW, Seow SL, et al. A Status Review of the Bioactive Activities of Tiger Milk Mushroom *Lignosus rhinocerotis* (Cooke) Ryvarden. *Front Pharmacol*. 2018;8:998. Published 2018 Jan 15. doi:10.3389/fphar.2017.00998
273 Lin LT, Tai CJ, Su CH, et al. The Ethanolic Extract of Taiwanofungus camphoratus (Antrodia camphorata) Induces Cell Cycle Arrest and Enhances Cytotoxicity of Cisplatin and Doxorubicin on Human Hepatocellular Carcinoma Cells. *Biomed Res Int*. 2015;2015:415269. doi:10.1155/2015/415269
274 Val, C.H., Brant, F., Miranda, A.S. *et al*. Effect of mushroom *Agaricus blazei* on immune response and development of experimental cerebral malaria. *Malar J* 14, 311 (2015).
275 Khatua, Somanjana et al. "Laetiporus sulphureus (Bull.: Fr.) Murr. as Food as Medicine." (2017).
276 Brandalise F, Cesaroni V, Gregori A, et al. Dietary Supplementation of *Hericium erinaceus* Increases Mossy Fiber-CA3 Hippocampal Neurotransmission and Recognition Memory in Wild-Type Mice. *Evid Based Complement Alternat Med*. 2017;2017:3864340. doi:10.1155/2017/3864340
277 Rossi P, Cesaroni V, Brandalise F, Occhinegro A, Ratto D, Perrucci F, Lanaia V, Girometta C, Orrù G, Savino E. Dietary Supplementation of Lion's Mane Medicinal Mushroom, Hericium erinaceus (Agaricomycetes), and Spatial Memory in Wild-Type Mice. Int J Med Mushrooms. 2018;20(5):485-494. doi:10.1615/IntJMedMushrooms.2018026241.
278 Spelman, Kevin & Sutherland, Elizabeth & Bagade, Aravind. (2017). Neurological Activity of Lion's Mane (Hericium erinaceus). Journal of Restorative Medicine. 6. 19-26. 10.14200/jrm.2017.6.0108.
279 Su H -H, Chu Y -C, Liao J -M, Wang Y -H, Jan M -S, Lin C-W, Wu C-Y, Tseng C-Y, Yen J -C and Huang S-S (2017) *Phellinus linteus* Mycelium Alleviates Myocardial Ischemia-Reperfusion Injury through Autophagic Regulation. *Front. Pharmacol.* 8:175. doi: 10.3389/fphar.2017.00175
280 Spelman, Kevin & Sutherland, Elizabeth & Bagade, Aravind. (2017). Neurological Activity of Lion's Mane (Hericium erinaceus). Journal of Restorative Medicine. 6. 19-26. 10.14200/jrm.2017.6.0108.
281 Eik, Lee-Fang & Naidu, Murali & David, Pamela & Kah Hui, Wong & Tan, Yee Shin & Sabaratnam, Vikineswary. (2012). Lignosus rhinocerus (Cooke) Ryvarden: A Medicinal Mushroom That Stimulates Neurite Outgrowth in PC-12 Cells. Evidence-based complementary and alternative medicine : eCAM. 2012. 320308. 10.1155/2012/320308.
282 Yang, Wenjian & Fang, Yong & Liang, Jin & Hu, Qiuhui. (2011). Optimization of ultrasonic extraction of Flammulina velutipes polysaccharides and evaluation of its acetylcholinesterase inhibitory activity. Food Research International. 44. 1269-1275. 10.1016/j.foodres.2010.11.027.
283 Yang, Wenjian & Yu, Jie & Zhao, Liyan & Ma, Ning & Fang, Yong & Pei, Fei & Mariga, Alfred & Hu, Qiuhui. (2015). Polysaccharides from Flammulina velutipes improve scopolamine-induced impairment of learning and memory of rats. Journal of Functional Foods. 18. 10.1016/j.jff.2015.08.003.
284 Anxiang, su & Yang, Wenjian & Zhao, Liyan & Pei, Fei & Zhong, Lei & Ma, Gaoxing & Hu, Qiuhui. (2018). Flammulina velutipes polysaccharides improve scopolamine-induced learning and memory impairment of mice by modulating gut microbiota composition. Food & Function. 9. 10.1039/C7FO01991B.
285 Chen W, Tan H, Liu Q, et al. A Review: The Bioactivities and Pharmacological Applications of *Phellinus linteus*. *Molecules*. 2019;24(10):1888. Published 2019 May 16. doi:10.3390/molecules24101888
286 Yi Z, Shao-Long Y, Ai-Hong W, et al. Protective Effect of Ethanol Extracts of Hericium erinaceus on Alloxan-Induced Diabetic Neuropathic Pain in Rats. *Evid Based Complement Alternat Med*. 2015;2015:595480. doi:10.1155/2015/595480
287 Nallathamby N, Phan CW, Seow SL, et al. A Status Review of the Bioactive Activities of Tiger Milk Mushroom *Lignosus rhinocerotis* (Cooke) Ryvarden. *Front Pharmacol*. 2018;8:998. Published 2018 Jan 15. doi:10.3389/fphar.2017.00998
288 Wang H, Fu Z, Han C. The Medicinal Values of Culinary-Medicinal Royal Sun Mushroom (Agaricus blazei Murrill). Evid Based Complement Alternat Med. 2013;2013:842619. doi: 10.1155/2013/842619.
289 Spelman, Kevin & Sutherland, Elizabeth & Bagade, Aravind. (2017). Neurological Activity of Lion's Mane (Hericium erinaceus). Journal of Restorative Medicine. 6. 19-26. 10.14200/jrm.2017.6.0108.
290 Girometta, Carolina. (2018). Antimicrobial properties of Fomitopsis officinalis in the light of its bioactive metabolites: a review. Mycology. 10. 1-8. 10.1080/21501203.2018.1536680.
291 Zhu, Jia-Shi & Halpern, Georges & Jones, Kenneth. (1998). The Scientific Rediscovery of a Precious Ancient Chinese Herbal Regimen: Cordyceps sinensis Part II. Journal of alternative and complementary medicine (New York, N.Y.). 4. 429-57. 10.1089/acm.1998.4.429.
292 Jesenak M, Hrubisko M, Majtan J, Rennerova Z, Banovcin P. Anti-allergic effect of Pleuran (β-glucan from Pleurotus ostreatus) in children with recurrent respiratory tract infections. Phytother Res. 2014 Mar;28(3):471-4. doi:10.1002/ptr.5020.
293 Harms, Manuela & Lindequist, Ulrike & Alresly, Zeyad & Wende, Kristian. (2013). Influence of the mushroom Piptoporus betulinus on human keratinocytes. Planta Medica. 79. 10.1055/s-0033-

1351998.

294 Rogers, Robert. (2014). Three Under-utilized Medicinal Polypores. Journal of American Herbalists Guild. Vol 12. No 2.

295 Spelman, Kevin & Sutherland, Elizabeth & Bagade, Aravind. (2017). Neurological Activity of Lion's Mane (Hericium erinaceus). Journal of Restorative Medicine. 6. 19-26. 10.14200/jrm.2017.6.0108.

296 Huang YL, Leu SF, Liu BC, Sheu CC, Huang BM. In vivo stimulatory effect of Cordyceps sinensis mycelium and its fractions on reproductive functions in male mouse. Life Sci. 2004 Jul 16;75(9):1051-62.

297 Kamo, Tsunashi et al. "Anti-inflammatory lanostane-type triterpene acids from Piptoporus betulinus." Journal of natural products 66 8 (2003): 1104-6 .

298 Sękara, Agnieszka & Kalisz, Andrzej & Grabowska, Aneta & Siwulski, Marek. (2015). Auricularia spp. - mushrooms as Novel Food and therapeutic agents - a review. Sydowia -Horn-. 67. 1-10. 10.12905/0380.sydowia67-2015-0001.

299 dith. (2014). European medicinal polypores – A modern view on traditional uses. Journal of Ethnopharmacology. 10.1016/j.jep.2014.04.030.

300 Masuda Y, Nakayama Y, Tanaka A, Naito K, Konishi M. Antitumor activity of orally administered maitake α-glucan by stimulating antitumor immune response in murine tumor. PLoS One. 2017 Mar 9;12(3):e0173621. doi:10.1371/journal.pone.0173621.

301 Balandaykin, Mikhail & Zmitrovich, Ivan. (2015). Review on Chaga Medicinal Mushroom, Inonotus obliquus (Higher Basidiomycetes): Realm of Medicinal Applications and Approaches on Estimating its Resource Potential. International Journal of Medicinal Mushrooms. 17. 95-104. 10.1615/IntJMedMushrooms.v17.i2.10.

302 Sun M, Zhao W, Xie Q, Zhan Y, Wu B. Lentinan reduces tumor progression by enhancing gemcitabine chemotherapy in urothelial bladder cancer. Surg Oncol. 2015 Mar;24(1):28-34. doi: 10.1016/j.suronc.2014.11.002.

303 Kobayashi H, Motoyoshi N, Itagaki T, Tabata K, Suzuki T, Inokuchi N. The inhibition of human tumor cell proliferation by RNase Pol, a member of the RNase T1 family, from Pleurotus ostreatus. Biosci Biotechnol Biochem.2013;77(7):1486-91

304 Petrović J, Stojković D, Reis FS, Barros L, Glamočlija J, Ćirić A, Ferreira IC, Soković M. Study on chemical, bioactive and food preserving properties of Laetiporus sulphureus (Bull.: Fr.) Murr. Food Funct. 2014 Jul 25;5(7):1441-51. doi: 10.1039/c4fo00113c.

305 Wong JY, Abdulla MA, Raman J, et al. Gastroprotective Effects of Lion's Mane Mushroom Hericium erinaceus (Bull.:Fr.) Pers. (Aphyllophoromycetideae) Extract against Ethanol-Induced Ulcer in Rats. Evid Based Complement Alternat Med. 2013;2013:492976. doi:10.1155/2013/492976

306 Noguchi M, Kakuma T, Tomiyasu K, Kurita Y, Kukihara H, Konishi F, Kumamoto S, Shimizu K, Kondo R, Matsuoka K. Effect of an extract of Ganoderma lucidum in men with lower urinary tract symptoms: a double-blind, placebo-controlled randomized and dose-ranging study. Asian J Androl. 2008 Jul;10(4):651-8.

307 Spelman, Kevin & Sutherland, Elizabeth & Bagade, Aravind. (2017). Neurological Activity of Lion's Mane (Hericium erinaceus). Journal of Restorative Medicine. 6. 19-26. 10.14200/jrm.2017.6.0108.

308 Rogers, Robert. (2014). Three Under-utilized Medicinal Polypores. Journal of American Herbalists Guild. Vol 12. No 2.

309 Nallathamby N, Phan CW, Seow SL, et al. A Status Review of the Bioactive Activities of Tiger Milk Mushroom Lignosus rhinocerotis (Cooke) Ryvarden. Front Pharmacol. 2018;8:998. Published 2018 Jan 15. doi:10.3389/fphar.2017.00998

310 Chen W, Tan H, Liu Q, et al. A Review: The Bioactivities and Pharmacological Applications of Phellinus linteus. Molecules. 2019;24(10):1888. Published 2019 May 16. doi:10.3390/molecules24101888

311 Patel, Yashvant et al. "Medicinal Properties of Pleurotus Species (Oyster Mushroom): A Review." (2012).

312 Patel, Yashvant et al. "Medicinal Properties of Pleurotus Species (Oyster Mushroom): A Review." (2012).

313 Alresly, Zeyad. (2015). Bioactive Triterpenes from the Fungus Piptoporus betulinus. Records of Natural Products.

314 Abdulla MA, Fard AA, Sabaratnam V, Wong KH, Kuppusamy UR, Abdullah N, Ismail S. Potential activity of aqueous extract of culinary-medicinal Lion's Mane mushroom, Hericium erinaceus (Bull.: Fr.) Pers. (Aphyllophoromycetideae) in accelerating wound healing in rats. Int J Med Mushrooms. 2011;13(1):33-9.

315 Chen, Pao-Huei & Weng, Yih-Ming & Yu, Zer-Ran & Koo, Malcolm & Wang, Bu-er. (2016). Extraction temperature affects the activities of antioxidation, carbohydrate-digestion enzymes, and angiotensin-converting enzyme of Pleurotus citrinopileatus extract. Journal of Food and Drug Analysis. 24. 10.1016/j.jfda.2016.02.005.

316 Irene Roncero-Ramos, Mónica Mendiola-Lanao, Margarita Pérez-Clavijo & Cristina Delgado-Andrade (2017) Effect of different cooking methods on nutritional value and antioxidant activity of

cultivated mushrooms, International Journal of Food Sciences and Nutrition, 68:3, 287-297, DOI: 10.1080/09637486.2016.1244662

317 Rogers, Robert. (2014). Three Under-utilized Medicinal Polypores. Journal of American Herbalists Guild. Vol 12. No 2.

318 Powell, Martin. *Medicinal Mushrooms: the Essential Guide*. Mycology Press, 2013.

319 Hobbs, Christopher. Medicinal Mushrooms III (1998), https://www.christopherhobbs.com/library/articles-on-herbs-and-health/medicinal-mushrooms-3/

320 Powell, Martin. *Medicinal Mushrooms: the Essential Guide*. Mycology Press, 2013.

321 Fungicopia, DIY Dual Extractions, Medicinal Mushrooms. *Fungicopia*. https://www.fungicopia.com/diy-dual-extraction

322 Hobbs, Christopher. Medicinal Mushrooms III (1998), https://www.christopherhobbs.com/library/articles-on-herbs-and-health/medicinal-mushrooms-3/

323 Powell, Martin. *Medicinal Mushrooms: the Essential Guide*. Mycology Press, 2013.

324 https://www.ncbi.nlm.nih.gov/pubmed/21698671

325 Hobbs, Christopher. Medicinal Mushrooms III (1998), https://www.christopherhobbs.com/library/articles-on-herbs-and-health/medicinal-mushrooms-3/

326 Powell, Martin. *Medicinal Mushrooms: the Essential Guide*. Mycology Press, 2013.

327 Fungicopia, DIY Dual Extractions, Medicinal Mushrooms. *Fungicopia*. https://www.fungicopia.com/diy-dual-extraction

328 Powell, Martin. *Medicinal Mushrooms: the Essential Guide*. Mycology Press, 2013.

329 https://www.annandachaga.com/pages/usage-dosage-chaga

330 Powell, Martin. *Medicinal Mushrooms: the Essential Guide*. Mycology Press, 2013.

331 Hobbs, Christopher. Medicinal Mushrooms III (1998), https://www.christopherhobbs.com/library/articles-on-herbs-and-health/medicinal-mushrooms-3/

332 Powell, Martin. *Medicinal Mushrooms: the Essential Guide*. Mycology Press, 2013.

333 Powell, Martin. *Medicinal Mushrooms: the Essential Guide*. Mycology Press, 2013.

334 Powell, Martin. *Medicinal Mushrooms: the Essential Guide*. Mycology Press, 2013.

335 Hobbs, Christopher. Medicinal Mushrooms III (1998), https://www.christopherhobbs.com/library/articles-on-herbs-and-health/medicinal-mushrooms-3/

336 Powell, Martin. *Medicinal Mushrooms: the Essential Guide*. Mycology Press, 2013.

337 Powell, Martin. *Medicinal Mushrooms: the Essential Guide*. Mycology Press, 2013.

Made in the USA
Middletown, DE
10 October 2023

40525788R00137